Notes
from the
Heart

A Celebration of
Traditional Irish Music

PJ CURTIS
FOREWORD BY PETER BROWNE

POOLBEG

Published in 1994 by
Torc
123 Baldoyle Industrial Estate,
Dublin 13, Ireland

© PJ Curtis 1994

Reprinted July 1999

The moral right of the author has been asserted.

A catalogue record for this book is available from the British Library.

ISBN 1 898142 0 76

Front cover photograph courtesy of Eamon Donovan
Back cover photographs courtesy of Na Píobairí Uilleann,
Gerard Linnane and Tommy Peoples
Cover design by Poolbeg Group Services Ltd
Set by Poolbeg Group Services Ltd in Garamond 10/13
Printed by The Guernsey Press Company Ltd, Vale,
Guernsey, Channel Islands.

Born in Clare, PJ Curtis is an award-winning record producer and radio presenter. He has produced thirty-three albums to date by a variety of artists, including Mary Black, Maura O'Connell, Stockton's Wing and Dolores Keane. He won the North American Independent Record Distributors (NAIRD) Record Producer Award both in 1990 and 1992 for his work on the Altan albums, *The Red Crow* and *Harvest Storm,* respectively. His RTE Radio One music series "Personal Best" earned him a Jacobs Radio Award in 1986. He also contributes artist profiles and album reviews to *Hot Press* and the New York *Irish-America* magazine.

Peter Browne is a noted uilleann piper and radio producer/presenter with several albums to his credit.

Acknowledgements

I wish to sincerely thank: Leo and Claire Hallisey; Patrick Farrelly; Pat Musick; Kathy Donehy; Cyril Ó Céirín and the North Clare Writers Group; my editor, Zoë O'Connor; my sister, Mary Moroney; the musicians and individuals, especially Sandy Harsch, who gave so freely of their time and for their unwavering support, encouragement and belief in the project and active help during the writing of this book.

Special thanks also to Peter Browne of RTE, Liam McNulty of Na Píobairí Uilleann, Harry Bradshaw and Nicholas Carolan of the Irish Traditional Music National Archives.

*This book is dedicated to my mother,
Sarah (1914–1989), who played the first
music I ever heard.*

Contents

FOREWORD

Traditional Irish music is many things nowadays—a multi-sided activity which has spread far beyond the shores of the country of its origin. Picture a German music-lover loading up a camper-van in preparation for a three-week holiday on the west coast of Ireland in search of good sessions—the perfect antidote to the Autobahn or the U-Bahn and the stress of life in a highly organised industrial society. That person may have been inspired to make the journey by hearing The Dubliners in Mannheim or by buying Micho Russell's tin whistle tutor after a concert in Munich. Then you find an Irish piper boarding the ferry at Rosslare, off to find adventure busking on the streets of Paris or Berlin—a journey undertaken, perhaps, with some disappointment at the meagre prospects of work in the land which has offered only the gangplank.

Then we have an American sound-engineer preparing a 24-track studio in San Francisco to record an instrumental break on the uilleann pipes for inclusion on the latest album by an internationally famous rock musician. Or a Frenchman who has come to Ireland to make a living as a skilled craftsman manufacturing sets of uilleann pipes with an order-book full of the names of hopeful would-be pipers from as far away as New Zealand. Students writing theses on flute-style, broadcasters preparing archive programmes on old long-gone fiddle players, committees searching for venues for competitions at a Fleadh Cheoil; all are part of this world.

It wasn't always so—I remember as a nine-year-old learner piper, being press-ganged into playing at the annual school concert—flushed with shame at this yearly activity in an urban primary school. At least one of the pupils in the class above me became a Boomtown Rat and that gained peer respectability in a way I never could. Years later, when I saw one of my former classmates at a traditional concert in Liberty Hall in Dublin, sitting enthusiastically in the front row, I allowed myself one "Well, now then!" spoken softly to myself.

Over one hundred years ago it wasn't so either—there were no radios, records or gigs—only rural people playing tunes for their own house-dances. Then came emigration, the 78 RPM disc, the céilí band, Comhaltas Ceoltóirí Éireann, Raidió Éireann, Seán Ó Riada, all the groups and all the excitement of the exponential growth in scope, variation, diversity, numbers of musicians and singers and somewhere in that time the advent of "listening" as opposed to "dance" music.

Perhaps some things have been lost or temporarily mislaid—the regional styles and the slow gentle tempo of playing—and it's not hard to see how. If a person gets into a car to drive from Dublin to Clare for a session of music, the car will flash at high speed through places where once the style was distinct from the playing in the next townland. If there's also a car radio or cassette-player, well, where's your regional style then? By the same process, a session in Ireland will now hear played newly composed Shetland Islands, Cajun, Bluegrass and French Canadian tunes—all good if they sound right to the players today.

You'll read all about how it happened and how it still happens and about all the people involved if you read this book. And the man writing it has music in his soul. PJ Curtis knew about "World Music" before it was spoken of. He grew up in County Clare, naturally hearing plenty of music in that time, and it made a deep impression on him. He discovered sounds outside of the traditional music of Ireland and physically, as well as musically, explored the world of emigration. But he told me of things falling into place one June on a visit home when he heard the great Clare piper, Willie Clancy, whom he describes in the the book as "a folk-poet of gigantic stature." Hearing Willie, he recognised the same soul and the same ability to speak with music as he heard in the great blues singers he also loves.

He also told me of the increasing difficulty in returning to England to work after each visit home with the prospect of yet another separation from the musical oasis of County Clare. The culmination of this was somewhere back in England, out driving in his car he heard across the airways on RTE Radio the piping of Liam Ó Floinn. In response to his question, "What am I doing here?" he left his job as an air-traffic controller and came home. Closer to the music, he was happier, and he came closer again by taking the job as a road-manager with The Bothy Band. I remember from this time his warm, gentle nature and from my short experience of the lifestyle of the travelling musician, if it was a job PJ undertook for money rather than pure love of music then I am myself a 5-string banjo!

The same love of music can be heard in the many records he has produced—they all have their own special acoustic sense and taste, and it carries forward into this book. As I read of the great burgeoning of music from the Sixties to today, much of it as seen from one closely involved, of the sadness and recording-experiences of the great émigré musicians of the early century, of the keenness for dancing in the countryside, of the the figureheads in County Clare music from yesterday and today, each representing an important strand in the story of Irish traditional music, I'm happy that he has written it. For others to enjoy, to learn, to refer to and to think about. Good on you, PJ.

Peter Browne

PART ONE

The Music
An Overview of Irish Traditional Music Since 1900

"Musical notes, with all their power to fire the blood and melt the heart, cannot be empty sounds and nothing more. No, they have escaped from some higher sphere. They are outporings of Eternal Harmony, the voice of angels, the Magnificat of Saints."

JG Frazer, *The Golden Bough*

Chapter One

A Brief History of Irish Traditional Music Since 1900

"Music is prophesy. Its styles and economic organisation are ahead of the rest of society because it explores, much faster than material reality can, the entire range of possibilities in a given code. It makes audible the new world that will gradually become visible....

It is not only the image of things, but the transcending of the everyday, the herald of the future. For that reason musicians, even when officially recognised, are dangerous, disturbing and subversive; for this reason it is impossible to separate their history from that of repression and surveillance."

Jacques Attali, *The Political Economy of Music*.

"It's not all that surprising that a nation whose language and culture was suppressed through centuries, should make music virtually the sole vehicle for its spirit, personality and aspiration."

John Waters, *The Irish Times*, 29 June 1993.

A frequently asked question is, what exactly is traditional music? Some time in the sixth century, Isodore of Seville described traditional music as, "music in which the sounds perish unless they are held in the memory of man."

According to the International Folk Music Council, traditional music is, "A product of a musical tradition of a community or region which has evolved through a process of oral transmission." Simply put, traditional music and song is the music of the people played by the people and transmitted orally from one generation to the next. It can also be termed folk music, though there is now a very clear distinction between what is termed folk and traditional music. Folk can refer to ballads and contemporary songs, usually accompanied by guitar. For example, in the American music tradition, Woody Guthrie, the early Bob Dylan, Joan Baez or John Prine might be classed as folk rather than traditional singers. So too might rural or urban blues singers Robert Johnson, Big Bill Broonzy, Muddy Waters or John Lee Hooker. Indeed, it could even be argued that Elvis Presley's early Fifties Memphis Sun records were string-band folk recordings. Here in Ireland, singers such as Mary Black, Christy Moore, Andy Irvine or Mick Daly of the group Any Old Time, could be termed folk singers; while Darach O'Catháin, Joe Heaney, Sarah, Rita and Dolores Keane, Len Graham, Mairéad and Tríona Ní Dhomhnaill or Mairéad Ní Mhaonaigh of the group Altan, would be classified as traditional singers. Though in some cases, it has to be said, the definitions become somewhat blurred.

Traditional Irish music comprises two broad categories—instrumental music and song. The instrumental music is mostly dance music and includes reels, jigs, hornpipes, polkas, slides and the like. The song category comprises mostly unaccompanied solo singing; though it is common now to hear traditional singers with various accompaniment. In poet Seán Golden's excellent essay on *Traditional Music and Contemporary Irish Literature* he writes, "Traditional music derives from the rhythms and quantities of the Irish language whose consonantal patterns and long vowels and intricate prosody mirror the intervals and rhythms of song and dance." Traditional music and song is rarely learned from a book. It passes from father to son, mother to daughter; from one generation to another; in an unbroken line which stretches back several centuries. In his seminal work, *Folk Music and Dances of Ireland*, Breandán Breathnach writes, "There is only one way to become a traditional player or singer, and that is by listening to genuine material performed in a traditional manner."

Dr John Barrow, writing in the 1983 *Scottish Review,* went even further, saying: "To have a healthy nation, in all forms of the arts, requires great attention to be paid to the traditional or indigenous arts of the nation."

The last thirty years has seen an extraordinary upsurge in interest in all forms of traditional, folk and acoustic music; not only in Ireland but also in England, Europe, Africa and the USA. So much so that it has earned, and is marketed internationally under, the title of "World Music." Groups such as The Chieftains, Planxty, The Bothy Band, De Danann and more recently Moving Hearts, Davy Spillane, Stockton's Wing, Sharon Shannon and Altan, have taken Irish traditional music in its different forms to practically every corner of the globe. Over the years, these bands have played to hundreds of thousands of fans of Irish music—many of them newly converted—on concert platforms from Houston to Hamburg, from Pittsburgh to Peking. The groups mentioned above are but the tip of the iceberg, spearheading the ever-swelling ranks of musicians playing and performing Irish traditional music, thus ensuring a place for the music alongside other forms of popular music today. Forty years ago all forms of traditional music, along with traditional singing and dancing, looked as if they were in grave danger of being added to the ever-growing extinct species listings. Today, in the early Nineties, Irish music lives and thrives in a way unimagined by even the most optimistic of observers of the music during these dark, bleak days of the Forties and Fifties. So how did this traditional music renaissance come about?

Pre-1920s

Prior to 1920 in Ireland, Irish traditional music of any kind being played on stage by more than one or two musicians was practically unheard of. Local musicians—fiddlers, pipers, concertina players—usually gathered in houses to play for groups of people who gathered to celebrate at Christmas-time, weddings and births or for the notorious American wakes. Otherwise music was provided by the professional travelling pipers or fiddlers. On long summer Sunday evenings in many parts of Ireland, travelling or local musicians and dancers congregated at crossroads in rural areas, though these gatherings often fell foul of the local clergy. Otherwise the individual fiddler, piper or singer learned at his parents' knee or collected from neighbouring musicians and carried these tunes and songs to be played or sung for him or herself or at small family gatherings. One early recording company, G&T (The Gramophone and Typewriter Co) recorded some uilleann pipe pieces in London; reputedly from Thomas Caroghan, according to the archivist and music historian, Nicholas Carolan. A few primitive recordings had been made, some as far back as 1898/9, at the annual Feis Cheoil held in Dublin. The piper Dinny Delaney had been recorded on cylinder, as had the legendary blind Kerry piper Micheál Cumba Ó Súilleabháin, who on hearing back the result of the recording process, proceeded to attack the infernal machine with his walking stick. Apart from these occasional recordings and Feis Cheoil annual gatherings, traditional music was localised; sparse in some areas, dead or dying in many others.

This situation contrasted greatly with that on the other side of the Atlantic. From the 1850s on, there existed in the East Coast cities a thriving Irish traditional music scene, with first-generation Irish fiddlers, flute-players and pipers in abundance. In Philadelphia, the famous uilleann pipe makers, the Taylor brothers, were active supplying pipers with sets of their finely crafted instruments, many of which are still being played by present-day pipers. In Chicago, the Police Chief and great scholar and collector of Irish music, Capt Francis O'Neill (born near Bantry, County Cork in 1839), had, by the 1870s, set about collecting and compiling his monumental contribution to traditional music, titled *The Music of Ireland*. It contained over 1,850 tunes and was published in 1903. A second edition, titled *The Dance Music of Ireland,* with 1,001 tunes, was published in 1907. It is generally accepted that no such comprehensive collection of Irish traditional music has since been published.

In New York, Philadelphia, Boston and Chicago a great many Irish traditional musicians who had emigrated there, such as fiddlers Michael Coleman, Paddy Killoran, Hugh Gillespie and James Morrison, concertina player William J Mullally and uilleann pipers Patrick J (Patsy) Touhy and Tom Ennis (born in Chicago of Irish parents; his father John, from County Kildare, was also a piper), were beginning to find full employment as professional musicians. They had also begun to record their music for posterity on the now classic 78 RPM discs, initially recorded for small independent labels such as New Republic, Celtic and Emerald. From the mid-Twenties on, the emerging stars recorded for Victor, Vocalion, Okeh, Decca, Columbia and Gennet, all major record-labels of the period. These shellac 78 RPM records (a huge improvement on the cylinder), shipped or brought to Ireland by the emigrant returning on holiday or for good, found an eager and appreciative audience and were to have an enormous influence on the future shape of traditional music back in Ireland. For the first time in history, a fiddler or piper in Kerry or Donegal could listen to, closely study and be influenced by the American-recorded music of Coleman, Killoran, Morrison or Touhey.

The 1920s and 1930s

As the 1920s progressed, the traditional music scene in Ireland looked bleak indeed. To hear genuine traditional music in its natural environment was the exception rather than the rule. There were precious few authentic traditional musicians being recorded in Ireland in the Twenties, and those who made it onto wax were generally issued on one of the three major recording companies—Columbia, Parlophone or His Master's Voice (HMV). One of the most outstanding and prolific musicians to be recorded during this period was the great uilleann pipe maker, teacher and player, the late Leo Rowsome. Born in Dublin in 1903 into a family steeped in uilleann pipe making and pipering, Leo was appointed Teacher of Uilleann Pipes at the Dublin College of Music at age nineteen, a post he held until his death in 1970. He was to achieve considerable fame as a piper, due mainly to his many appearances on Irish radio and his numerous 78 RPM record releases during the Twenties and Thirties for the HMV, Columbia, Decca and lesser-known Broadcast labels. (Prior to 1937, when companies set up recording facilities in Dublin, traditional musicians had to travel to London to record.)

For several decades, until his sudden death in 1970, Leo Rowsome's marvellous music thrilled and moved fans of Irish music everywhere and his rich, dynamic legato piping, played on his full-toned and perfectly-tuned instrument, became the yardstick against which most other younger pipers were judged.

Another uilleann piper to record during the late Twenties and early Thirties was the Waterford-born piper Liam Walsh, who learned from Leo Rowsome's father Willie and recorded a number of 78s for the Columbia and Decca labels. Though there were other traditional musicians making 78s in the same period, such as the Fingal Trio, which featured uilleann piper James Ennis (father of Séamus Ennis), Frank O'Higgins (fiddle) and John Cawley (flute) and the Dublin-based Belhavel Trio (featuring piper Ned O'Gorman and Tom and Joe Liddy on accordion and fiddle, respectively), the majority of Irish 78 issues were of of the "Irish Tenor" variety or novelty items. The commercial value of releasing authentic forms of traditional music had not as yet been fully realised by the recording companies active in Ireland at that time. During this period, it's true to say that in the length and breadth of Ireland, in any household with a love of traditional music and a wind-up gramophone, one was certain to find a number of these artists' records or the highly-prized Coleman, Morrison, Killoran, Touhey or Flanagan Brothers American 78 RPM records.

During this post-Civil War period (1922 on), widespread emigration continued to ravage the countryside, resulting in a great many, musicians included, departing to England and Australia but primarily to the United States. In the words of west Clare fiddle player Junior Crehan, "The young women left the land and they were followed by the young men. Then the musicians left to follow them. There was nobody left, why wouldn't they go? They had nobody left to play to." As the Thirties progressed, the homely house-dances were outlawed in most areas of rural Ireland. The punitive Public Dance Hall Act of 1935 was introduced to control the commercial dance-halls which had begun to spring up around the country and was ultimately used to eradicate the house-dance. Irish set-dancing, which had been on the decline since the turn of the century, thereafter practically ceased to be an integral part of the social fabric of rural Ireland. Many musicians, deprived of a natural platform, laid aside their instruments, having no further use for them. This development, coupled with the growing numbers emigrating, resulted in the further decline of the music. At the close of the decade it looked as if the music of the countryside had begun to slip silently from folk memory. It might very well have done so, had it not been for a handful of dedicated individuals in Dublin, in Cork city and in isolated pockets around the country— Leitrim, Roscommon and more especially west of the Shannon, in Counties Donegal, Sligo, Mayo, Galway, Kerry and Clare.

The 1940s and 1950s

The cold and impersonal atmosphere of the dance-halls in the towns and the villages did, however, give rise to an alternative platform for traditional music. This emerged in the form of the céilí band. A typical céilí band would consist of a couple of fiddles, flute, accordion, concertina and banjo. Drums and piano, and later even tenor saxophone and double-bass, were added to augment the overall sound. Similar developments had occurred in America among the predominately fiddle string bands in Texas and Oklahoma, giving rise to the emergence of the musical style now referred to as Western or Texas Swing. This then was the typical céilí band line-up which was to play for and entertain set-dancers in the clergy-controlled parochial halls up and down the country. Seán Ó Riada, who abhorred the céilí band sound, was later to comment

in his radio series, *Our Musical Heritage,* that the sound
the céilí band made had "...as much relationship to music
as the buzzing of a bluebottle in an upturned jam-jar." Had
Ó Riada voiced this opinion at any of the packed céilí
dances the length of the country in the Fifties or Sixties, it
is doubtful if he would have come away unscathed. While
imported jazz and swing music and modern dance (the
foxtrot, the exotic tango and rumba and for the
exhibitionist, the jitterbug) swept the land in the Forties
and early Fifties, particularly in the larger towns and cities,
the Sunday night céilí dance held its own in the rural
areas. Again, this tradition was strongest in counties west
of the Shannon, where dancers elected their own hierarchy
of céilí bands. Among the most popular of these were the
Ballinakill Céilí Band from east Galway (who had recorded
78s in London as far back as 1931), the Austin Stack Céilí
Band, the Gallowglass Céilí Band, the Kilfenora and the
Tulla Céilí Bands from County Clare and the Aughrim
Slopes Céilí Band from County Galway. These bands
dominated the Irish dancing scene, not only in rural
Ireland but also in many English cities such as Liverpool,
London, Luton and Birmingham. Further afield, in the
American cities, the bands regularly visited to play for the
thousands of Irish men and women who had emigrated
there in the Forties and Fifties.

By the late Fifties, the world had changed and Ireland
had changed with it. The popularity of the céilí band
suffered a setback with the arrival of Elvis Presley and rock
n' roll, mainly through the medium of radio and the arrival
on the scene of the Showbands, dance-bands that
specialised in recreating rock n' roll and the popular hits of
the period. Many of the surviving céilí bands worked only
at Easter or Christmas-time, when a céilí might be held for
returning emigrants in the local parish hall. It then became
possible to hear authentic traditional music and song on

Irish national radio. The man most responsible for ensuring that the public was exposed to the finest traditional musicians and singers from town and country was music-collector and broadcaster Ciarán Mac Mathúna, whose ground-breaking weekly radio programmes of traditional music, *A Job of Journeywork* and *Ceolta Tíre*, became essential listening for anyone with even the slightest interest in the real thing. Also essential listening in the Fifties was *As I Roved Out*, a weekly radio programme of traditional music and song presented on the BBC by the great uilleann piper/singer/folklorist and collector, Séamus Ennis. Séamus's superb *As I Roved Out* never gained the listenership it deserved, mainly due to the fact that BBC transmission signals did not penetrate to all areas and, to most people in the Republic, the BBC was regarded as a foreign radio station. Ciarán's and Séamus's programmes proved that Irish traditional music and song—though reported ill and in many cases near death in some areas—was alive and well in selected pockets around the country. Through both men's radio work there grew a lively and informed interest in traditional music and song. Home-based recording companies slowly began to respond, resulting in Irish-issued records of traditional artists becoming commercially available nationwide. Records, initially 78s, then EPs and finally LPs by the Kilfenora or the Tulla Céilí Bands and solo recordings by musicians such as the northern fiddle virtuoso Seán McGuire and Paddy O'Brien, the great accordion player from east Tipperary, could be found in the homes of most lovers of traditional music in every county in Ireland. The distinction of being the first traditional musicians in Ireland to record an LP record fell to members of the east Clare-based Tulla Céilí Band, the legendary fiddlers Paddy Canny and PJ Hayes, the multi-talented instrumentalist Peadar O'Loughlin on fiddle and flute and Bridie Lafferty on piano. This superb LP, entitled *All Ireland Champions* (Shamrock Records), captured the pure essence of Irish traditional music at its very best. Today, almost forty years after its original release, the album remains a much-sought item by collecters and lovers of traditional music alike. As the Fifties drew to a close, it has to be said, one was more likely to encounter Irish traditional music in a "live" concert in the Irish-run bars and dance-halls of Kilburn, Camden Town, Chicago or the Bronx than in many counties of Ireland.

The 1960s

Some time in the early to mid-Sixties, almost without warning it seemed, Ireland saw a significant upsurge of interest in traditional music. So much so that by 1965, the beginnings of a mini-revolution in Irish music was under way. Many reasons have been put forward to explain this extraordinary resurgence in the music at that time. The regular radio programmes of traditional music (the BBC's *As I Roved Out,* compiled and presented by Séamus Ennis, and Radió Éireann's *Ceolta Tíre* and *A Job of Journeywork,* compiled and presented by Ciarán Mac Mathúna), did much to help the music survive and more importantly, helped expose the music to a wider, and previously indifferent, listening audience. Comhaltas Ceoltóirí Éireann (CCE), which had been founded in 1951 to foster and encourage traditional music and song, and had worked ceaselessly in that area, had also added a tremendous impetus to this new growth of interest. The Fleadh Cheoil (Festival of Music), the premier Irish music festival of that period, annually drew hundreds of musicians and thousands of followers to different venues around the country to play, compete and enjoy the convivial atmosphere of the gatherings. The mid-Sixties also saw the dawning of an era of unprecedented economic growth in Ireland. For the first time in several hundred years, a generation of young Irish men and women did not have to consider emigration as their only option. A dynamic new energy found release in this seemingly new Ireland, growing in confidence almost daily. That confidence permeated not only the business sector but also the arts in all forms. For one golden moment, everything was hopeful, everything was possible.

Yet the prime cause for the rise of interest in indigenous folk and traditional music was not to be found in these islands but rather in the United States. The folk boom in the States had been presided over by the likes of The Weavers, Pete Seeger, the Kingston Trio and Moe Asch and his Folkways Record label in the Fifties. The early Sixties produced Peter, Paul and Mary, Joan Baez, Dave Van Ronk and Bob Dylan. This movement, which on the East Coast centred in and around New York's Greenwich Village, had made folk heroes of four young Irishmen in white Aran sweaters who belted out the folk songs and ballads of their native land with moving passion, pride and manly gusto. These were the Clancy Brothers from County Tipperary and Tommy Makem from County Armagh, whose fame and popularity made them folk superstars both at home and abroad. When they returned home to great critical acclaim it seemed that practically overnight they initiated the ballad boom in Ireland. Soon ballads, folk and traditional songs were to be heard, sung alongside the pop songs of the day, in pubs and folk clubs throughout the land. The folk and ballad boom in Ireland went in tandem with a similar upsurge of interest in the UK spearheaded by Ewan McColl and Peggy Seeger, the Copper family, The Young Tradition, The Watersons, Dave Swarbrigg and Martin Carthy, Donovan and Ray and Archie Fisher. The late Sixties saw the phenomenon of a ballad group from Ireland's capital city, The Dubliners—featuring the late Luke Kelly, Ronnie Drew, the late Ciarán Burke, Barney McKenna and John Sheehan—make their appearance in the British Top Ten charts in 1967. They did so with *Seven Drunken Nights* (Major-Minor label), a ballad which also found its way into the American folk and blues tradition. (Ref: *Wake Up Baby* by blues-harmonica player Sonny Boy Williamson, recorded in Chicago in the mid-Fifties.) The Dubliners had to wait another twenty years before they hit the pop charts again, which they did with the London-Irish group, The Pogues, led by the irrepressible Shane McGowan, reworking a raucous version of the old chestnut *The Irish Rover,* a rip-roaring ballad made famous by both The Dubliners and the Clancy Brothers in the Sixties. Another Irish ballad was to crash into the UK Hit Parade in 1973, when Dublin rockers Thin Lizzy, led by Phil Lynott, adapted the old ballad, *Whiskey in the Jar*. The Dubliners were followed by a plethora of acoustic groups, many of whom went on to achieve great fame, if not fortune, as folk superstars.

One group who achieved both were the Furey Brothers and Davey Arthur. The genesis of this group was in the huge reputation built in England in the Sixties and later in Germany by the brothers Eddie (guitar and vocals) and Finbar Furey (uilleann pipes, whistle and vocals). One of their first single record releases in the UK, *Her Father Didn't Like Me Anyway,* writen by Gerry Rafferty, found its way into the charts and into the hearts of thousands of fans through pop and rock radio programmes on the BBC. For the Furey Brothers (later to be joined by their cousin Davey Arthur), it was just the beginning, with a string of hit records and concert successes to follow throughout the Seventies and Eighties.

Among the best known of the other emerging groups were Sweeney's Men (which featured Andy Irvine, Terry

Woods and Johnny Moynihan), The Johnstons (featuring Mick Moloney, Paul Brady and Lucy and Adrienne Johnston), The Ludlows and Emmett Spiceland. The latter had Donal Lunny in its ranks, the man who was to emerge as one of the major driving forces in the Irish music scene in the Seventies. Solo singers, too, were having considerable commercial success in Ireland with ballads. Johnny McEvoy was one such singer who achieved pop-star status in the late Sixties with his release of *Goodbye Mursheen Durkin* when it battled its way to the top of the charts alongside The Beatles and The Rolling Stones. An early version of this song, *Molly Durkin,* was recorded in New York in 1929 by Murty Rabitte, an emigrant from Oranmore in County Galway.

While the balladeers and their ballads gained enthusiasts and new converts daily, another branch of the traditional tree had been growing rapidly under the genius of Seán Ó Riada. In the Fifties, Ó Riada's restless musical spirit had explored and experimented with new music forms. In 1961, with his group, Ceoltóirí Chualann, made up of Dublin-based traditional musicians including Martin Fay and John Kelly (fiddles and concertina), Sonny Brogan and Éamonn de Buitléar (accordion), Michael Tubridy (flute), Paddy Moloney (pipes), Ronny McShane (bodhrán), Seán Ó Sé (vocals) and Ó Riada himself on piano, harpsichord and bodhrán, he set about reviving the eighteenth-century harp music of O'Carolan and other old tunes, airs, songs and pieces. His presentation of this new-formula traditional music was greeted with both critical and public acclaim. Ó Riada's musical vision of merging uilleann pipes, fiddles, flute, concertina and bodhrán with the more classical sound of harp and harpsichord sign-posted new directions for many younger traditional musicians. Ó Riada was, in the words of musician Micheál Ó Súilleabháin (who held the position in the Department of Music in University College, Cork, once held by Ó Riada himself and who was recently appointed Professor of Music at the University of Limerick), "above all else, a composer. It is only when we view him in this light that we can hope to unravel the many facets of the man as performer, composer, ensemble director, educator and broadcaster. As a composer, he was seeking a new form of Irish art music. As a musician, he now spanned the three faces of the contemporary music scene in Ireland—jazz/pop, European art and traditional."

His work as a broadcaster was equally pioneering. With the aid of west Clare fiddler John Kelly, Ó Riada scoured the country to record the different regional styles of traditional music and song still extant. In 1963, Ó Riada presented the results of his and John Kelly's labours in a fifteen-week Radió Éireann series titled *Our Musical Heritage*, a comprehensive and enlightening aural picture of the country's diverse traditional musical heritage. The series was considered to be a breakthrough as it made the general public aware for the first time of the inherent beauty, the richness and the complexity of traditional music.

Though he had his critics, Ó Riada, who died in 1971, was hailed as an innovator and was indeed seen by many as a genius and the saviour of an aspect of our musical heritage which was about to slip from folk memory. By 1968, Ceoltóirí Chualann had ceased to perform as a unit, though they did come together to record the celebrated live album for Gael-Linn, *Ó Riada sa Gaiety*.

In 1963, a group calling themselves The Chieftains issued their ground-breaking debut album, *Chieftains 1,* on the Claddagh label. Led by founder member, uilleann piper Paddy Moloney, along with Seán Keane and Martin Fay (fiddles), Seán Potts (tin whistle), Michael Tubridy (flute), Derek Bell (harp) and Peadar Mercier (bodhrán and bones), the group retained and developed many of Ó Riada's musical concepts. Over twenty-five years on, The Chieftains, having undergone some personnel changes (Seán Potts, Michael Tubridy and Peadar Mercier departed from the group to be replaced by the grand master of traditional flute, Matt Molloy and singer/bodhrán player Kevin Conniffe), are now the most travelled and best-known group playing Irish traditional music in its purest form. They have played to full houses in the major concert halls throughout the world, from the Albert Hall to Carnegie Hall and the Sydney Opera House. They have also provided music for several international films including *Barry Lyndon* (for which they won an Oscar), *The Purple Taxi* and *The Grey Fox* (*The Year of the French* and *Ballad of the Irish Horse* for TV) and have to date over 20 albums to their credit. Over the three decades their achievements have, to say the least, been considerable. In 1985, they were the first group to take Irish traditional music to China and South-East Asia.

In March 1993 they were awarded two Grammies, one for for their RCA album *Another Country*, voted Best Contemporary Folk Album, recorded in Nashville, Tennessee, with such country-music luminaries as Ricky Skaggs, Chet Atkins, Don Williams and Emmylou Harris, and one for *An Evening Live at the Grand Opera House, Belfast*, voted Best Contemporary Folk Album. There is no doubt that on a global scale, The Chieftains, along with U2, look set to continue to be Irish music's most able, respected and best-loved ambassadors.

The 1970s and 80s

Irish traditional music has come a long way in the last three decades. In the Seventies, certainly a vintage decade for the music and song, musicians with no roots in traditional music began to take an interest in the music. Several of these went on to form groups and play in the growing number of clubs and the "singing pubs" springing up around the country. These establishments initially became all the rage in Dublin but soon spread throughout the country. They offered, as *The Independent* commented at the time, "Rousing roof-ripping Irish ballad sessions," attracting a clientele which previously may have shown little or no interest in Irish music. With the exception of the legendary O'Donoghue's Pub in Dublin's Merrion Row and a few other select establishments, the majority of the "singing pubs" offered little by way of authentic traditional music, or, for that matter, songs or ballads. What they offered were "rip-roaring" evenings of bawdy, boozy ballad-singing, where anybody who could sing a note, or strum a guitar or banjo, could take an active part. It was all great fun, generating a huge business for the pubs. An *Irish Times* report of the day commented on the "singing pubs" phenomenon, observing that "a kind of floating population of voices, guitars, tin whistles, spoons and banjos is now welcomed in pubs which a few years ago unceremoniously bounced anyone merry enough to lift an isolated voice in song." The writer Donald S Connery, in his book, *The Irish* (Arrow Books, 1972), suggests that the "Ballad Boom" was Ireland's new "Popular Music" which in the Ireland of the day "meant more than Sinatra or even The Beatles." He also suggests that the highly commercialised world of the "singing pubs" were "Ireland's answer to the night-clubs and discotheques of London, Paris and Rome."

There has always been a thriving community of active traditional musicians in Cork city and county. Na File, a trio formed in Cork city in the late Sixties, emerged to gain a reputation for purity, excellence and virtuoso musicianship. The group, made up of Tomás Ó Canainn on uilleann pipes, Tom Barry on tin whistle and Matt Cranitch on fiddle, recorded their debut album for the Cork-based Mercier label before going on to release three subsequent albums for the Outlet and Dolphin labels, respectively. Following the group's demise in the late Seventies, Tomás Ó Canainn, the author of a book on traditional music, went on to record a number of solo albums for the Outlet label, while fiddler Matt Cranitch went on to form Any Old Time with Dave Hennessey on melodeon and Mick Daly on vocals, banjo and guitar. The group's debut album on the Mulligan label, simply titled *Any Old Time* (LUN047), is a gem, showcasing Cranitch and Hennessey's sublime marriage of fiddle and melodeon coupled with Mick Daly's soulful singing. The album remains as fresh and exciting today as when it was released in the late Seventies.

The early Seventies saw new musical liaisons being formed and as traditional Irish music, contemporaty folk, American and mid-European influences began to coalesce, it seemed almost inevitable that a new sound would emerge.

The arrival of the group Planxty on the scene confirmed this. The marriage of pure traditional tunes to the folk and ballad style worked perfectly in the hands of Liam Ó Floinn (uilleann pipes), Christy Moore (vocals/guitar), Andy Irvine (mandola/vocals) and Donal Lunny (bouzouki/bodhrán and vocals). The individuals had first come together, along with Kevin Conniffe on bodhrán and Clive Collins on fiddle, for the recording of the seminal album *Prosporous,* for the Tara label. Following the success of the album, Moore, Lunny, Irvine and Ó Floinn decided to form a group. Having considered the name Clad (the individuals' initials), they wisely settled for the group name Planxty— meaning a toast in praise of a person or thing.

The colourful and tasteful blending of the various stringed instruments, added to the stunning virtuosity of

PJ Curtis

Liam Ó Floinn's uilleann piping and the rich and varied vocal styles of Irvine, Moore and Lunny, made Planxty the heroes of the clubs, campuses and finally the concert halls both at home and abroad. Under the creative guidance of Donal Lunny, coupled with the considerable individual talents of Moore, Irvine and Ó Floinn, Planxty sought and found new ways to present old material. Their innovative, dynamic arrangements, their rock group-like appearance and their collective personal charisma made them the darlings of the folk, folk-rock and contemporary circuits in Ireland, Britain and Europe. Their superb debut album, simply titled *Planxty* (a.k.a. *The Black Album*), released in 1972, set the music scene alight on its way into the Irish Top Twenty Charts and into the hearts of traditional and folk music lovers the world over. Over twenty years on, *The Black Album,* and indeed all Planxty's subsequent album and compilation releases, are still among the most sought-after Irish albums. When Planxty were not filling halls, they returned to play as individuals at informal sessions with other musicians in and around Dublin. Seán Keane of The Chieftains, Liam Ó Floinn and Matt Molloy, later of The Bothy Band, could be found playing at impromptu get-togethers, in Dublin or Clare, exchanging tunes and ideas. At other Dublin sessions, in O'Donoghue's Pub in Merrion Row or in Slattery's of Capel Street, the fiddles of Tommy Peoples, Paddy Glackin and James and John Kelly along with Peter Browne's pipes or Paul Brady's mandolin or guitar, enthralled listeners—most of them young folk-music, traditional and rock fans—with such magical, electrifying music as to make time and space stand still.

In the late Seventies, Micheál Ó Súilleabháin was to write of this period: "The arrival of groups such as The Chieftains and Planxty—later to have a more viable successor in The Bothy Band—opened the music to an even younger audience. This new group involvement is the single greatest factor in the present international interest in Irish traditional music. It is because of this that musicians like Micho Russell can now sit alone on a stage in Germany and receive tumultuous applause for playing his tin whistle in his own pure style."

While the pub ballads merged with traditional piping and fiddle tunes, another more serious approach to traditional singing was being evolved by a group calling themselves Skara Brae. The mixing of harmony singing in Irish with clavichord and Bert Jansch/John Renbourne-style guitar playing brought a fresh dimension to the traditional and folk-group sound and resulted in a penetrating influence on several groups which were to follow. Skara Brae consisted of Tríona, Mairéad and Micheál Ó Domhnaill and Dáithí Sproule. Their only album, *Skara Brae* (Gael-Linn, 1974), is without doubt a milestone. The Ó Domhnaills' songs and singing style drew on the Sean-Nós (Old Style or Tradition) of their native north-west Donegal. Tríona and Micheál went on to join The Bothy Band, taking with them a great wealth of songs, most of them collected from their paternal aunt, the late Neíllí Ní Dhomhnaill from Rannafast in County Donegal.

Literally down the road from Neíllí lives the Ó Braonáin (Brennan) family, also the inheritors of a rich musical heritage. Máire Ní Bhraonáin (harp and vocals), with brothers Ciarán (bass) and Pól (flute) and their youthful twin uncles Noel and Pádraig Ó Dúgáin (guitars), developed yet another contemporary-folk, even jazz-tinged, approach to the playing and singing of traditional music and song. Calling themselves Clannad, their stylistic approach, which has been described by Nuala O'Connor in her book *Bringing It All Back Home* as…"moody, ethereal and atmospheric," today represents for many people the New Age Celtic Twilight sound, evoking magic, mystery and mysticism. Clannad went on to build a huge reputation, initially as a folk supergroup and later as a rock supergroup in the wake of their initial pop hit, *Harry's Game*. Their younger sister, Enya, who appeared with the group on their 1982 album, *Fuaim* (Tara), went on to become a major international recording artist in her own right, with three world-wide hit albums to her credit.

In 1973 a group of Galway-based musicians calling themselves De Danann burst onto the music scene, concentrating their sound on the weaving and blending of Frankie Gavin's fiery, positively virtuoso fiddle playing with the equally fiery and hard-driving bouzouki of Alec Finn, the banjo of Charlie Piggott, the accordion of Jackie Daly and the Gene Krupa of the bodhrán Johnny "Ringo" McDonagh. The vocals on their debut album were provided by the great Dolores Keane, the diva of traditional singers, whose roots (like those of the Ó Domhnaills) were buried deep in a long line of traditional family singing. Most of her songs, and her superbly controlled singing style, were learned from her aunts, Sarah and Rita Keane of Caherlistrane, County Galway, whose two-as-one soulful, melancholic singing has to be heard to be fully appreciated. In the twenty-odd years since De Danann's eruption onto the music scene, there have been many changes of personnel—singer Dolores Keane was replaced first by Andy Irvine, then by Johnny Moynihan, who was replaced in turn by Maura O'Connell, who was later replaced by Mary Black, who was followed by Eleanor Shanley. Colm Murphy replaced Johnny McDonagh on bodhrán and Máirtín O'Connor took over from Jackie Daly on accordion. Regardless of those changes, the Gavin/Finn fiddle/bouzouki relationship has remained the central and most dominant sound of this classic traditional group.

As time passed, new group formations began to appear.

Skara Brae had split, Micheál Ó Domhnaill joining forces for a time with singer-guitarist Mick Hanly to form Monroe. Micheál's sister Tríona joined the little-known, short-lived but influential 1691, which harnessed the talents of Matt Molloy on flute, Peter Browne on pipes, Tommy Peoples on fiddle and Liam Weldon on vocals and bodhrán. In 1973, Donal Lunny parted company with Planxty, to be replaced by Johnny Moynihan. Later in 1974, Paul Brady was to join Planxty's line-up.

1975 saw the arrival of The Bothy Band, one of the most exciting combinations of Irish music talents ever assembled. Donal Lunny and Tríona and Micheál Ó Domhnaill combined with undisputed master of the traditional flute, Matt Molloy, fiddler Paddy Glackin (later replaced by Tommy Peoples, in turn replaced by Kevin Burke), and uilleann piper Paddy Keenan. Paddy's breathtaking piping style encompassed all the hereditary skills of the travelling pipers of old, playing with powerful ease, imaginative flair, passion and vitality. The front-line powerhouse trio of Keenan's pipes, Peoples' fiddle and Molloy's flute resulted in the release of an awesome and explosive musical energy that has rarely been equalled. Their devastating live concert appearances at home and abroad, coupled with their ground-breaking album releases, won scores of new fans for the Bothies. Many of these fans were rock or pop music lovers with no previous interest in, or indeed knowledge of, Irish traditional music. Witnessing the group live, in full spate, was an experience never be forgotten. *Melody Maker* critic Colin Irwin summed up this phenomenon: "The Bothy Band were instantly lethal. You knew instinctively and immediately that here was a band on another planet to all the others. Hearing them for the first time was a bit on the 'Where were you on the night Kennedy was assassinated?' lines. Ireland's most exciting folk band ever."

Unquestionably, their innovative fire-brand approach to the music represented, as did Planxty's mixing of traditional and contemporary, a supreme example of the urbanisation of Irish rural music. A good analogy of this urbanisation of a traditional rural music can be found in the evolution of the American Blues, from its early acoustic rural Delta roots to its electrified, high-powered, high-energy urban offspring to be heard in Memphis, Detroit or Chicago.

By 1976, other dramatic changes had come about. Planxty had decided to call it a day; Dolores Keane had departed from De Danann, to be replaced by Andy Irvine. And so the wheel continued to turn. Christy Moore, Paul Brady and Mick Hanly pursued solo careers. Prior to going solo Paul Brady joined Andy Irvine for the recording of their much-celebrated album for the Mulligan label. New groups began to appear seemingly daily. Eddie and Finbar Furey, who had been playing professionally as a family unit since the Sixties, expanded the group to include their brother George and cousin Davey Arthur. They went on to build a large following, especially in Germany, where they worked almost continuously. Other groups, such as Oisín, Cork's Stoker's Lodge (featuring ebullient balladeer Jimmy Crowley), General Humbert (featuring Mary Black's debut on commercial record) and Stockton's Wing from Ennis, County Clare, began to make their presence felt with strong album releases and live performances in international pubs and clubs and on folk festival stages.

As the Seventies came to a close The Bothy Band played their last live gig and left an enduring legend. Planxty had re-formed with Matt Molloy added to the line-up of Moore, Irvine and Ó Floinn to tour and regularly headline the annual folk festivals held at Ballisodare in County Sligo and in Lisdoonvarna in Clare. For many, the group's old magic had dissipated somewhat. Gone too, or about to depart, were many of their fans—to London, Boston, New York, San Francisco or Sydney to seek employment. Never far from the Irish economic landscape, the grim spectre of rising unemployment once again began to take its toll as massive emigration resumed.

In the early Eighties in Dublin rumours of the formation of a new supergroup were in the air. That group finally emerged in 1981 with a barnstorming debut album coupled with a series of positively devastating live performances. Moving Hearts was the dream-child of Donal Lunny and Christy Moore, who felt that there was tremendous potential in the merging of traditional music with contemporary electric rock. It was a marriage of styles which had, after all, been successfully achieved in England by Steeleye Span and Fairport Convention in the late Sixties and to some degree by Irish folk-rockers, Horslips, in the Seventies.

The Hearts, with Lunny and Moore (Mick Hanly, followed by Flo McSweeney, were later to join the band as vocalists), piper Davy Spillane, ace sax-man Keith Donald, guitarist Declan Sinnott (now with Mary Black), bassist Eoghan O'Neill and drummer Matt Kelligan, proved the perfect vehicle. In one move, Donal Lunny had taken Irish traditional themes to the rock concert-stage and introduced them to an audience weaned on the American and English rock of the preceding decades. Four years and three albums later, Moving Hearts, unquestionably the most talented, exciting and innovative traditional-rock band ever to come out of Ireland, decided in September 1984 to call it a day, unable to survive in the brutal world of rock economics. Five days after their break-up the Hot Press/Stag Awards gave them a special award, "For Brilliant Musicianship, For Live performances of Extraordinary Intensity and For Giving Their All." No band in Ireland deserved it more. Their only instrumental album, *The Storm*

(Tara Records), recorded between December 1984 and May 1985, featuring a second piper, Declan Masterson, and guitarist Greg Boland, was released to great critical acclaim. *The Storm* continues to be a best-selling album and remains a milestone of Irish recording.

While Christy Moore and Davy Spillane pursued solo careers, Donal Lunny went on to concentrate on record production, occasionally emerging from the recording studios to perform at rare Moving Hearts get-togethers. His appearance at the Seán Ó Riada Retrospective concert at the National Concert Hall, Dublin, on 25 April 1987 resulted in the subsequent release of a live album on the Gael-Linn label. The album, simply entitled *Donal Lunny*, captures both the spirit and the excitement of the night and the brilliance of the ensemble of fine traditional musicians put together by Donal especially for the performance. On this album, Donal was joined by Nollaig Ní Chathasaigh (fiddle), Cormac Breathnach (flute), Seán Óg Potts (uilleann pipes), Arty McGlynn (guitar), Donal's brother Manus Lunny (bouzouki) and Damien Quinn and Steve White (percussion).

Meanwhile, both Moving Hearts uilleann pipers Davy Spillane and Declan Masterson had opted for solo careers. Dublin piper Masterson subsequently released a solo album, *End of the Harvest* (Gael-Linn), on which he displays his skill as a piper and his burgeoning talent as an arranger and composer. Davy Spillane formed his own band, issuing several albums, among them *Atlantic Bridge, Out of the Air* and *Shadow Hunter* (Tara Records). He has established himself as a much sought-after session musician of international repute, guesting on albums by Chris Rea, Elvis Costello, Kate Bush, Stevie Winwood and the African artist, Baba Maal.

Few professional groups playing Irish traditional music in the Seventies, with the exception of De Danann,

Clannad, the Furey Brothers, The Chieftains, and a handful of other bands, survived into and through the Eighties. As witnessed with The Bothy Band, many groups succumbed to the pressures of touring and recording and making ends meet in the hard-edged world of the commercial music business. One group that did survive the lean Eighties was Stockton's Wing. The Wing, as they are affectionately called, originally grew from the ashes of the group Inchiquin in the late Seventies. From this group, which featured Noel Hill and Tony Linnane, came the Clare banjo-player Kieran Hanrahan and singer/guitarist Tony Callanan from east Galway. Along with fellow Clare musician Paul Roche, Kieran Hanrahan's cousin, on flute, fiddler Maurice Lennon from County Leitrim and Tommy Hayes on bodhrán, Hanrahan and Callanan formed the group Stockton's Wing in 1981 and recorded their debut album for Tara Records. The strong Clare flavour created by Kieran Hanrahan's banjo and Paul Roche's flute, peppered by the stylish fiddle playing of Maurice Lennon, a member of the famous Lennon family, brought an equally strong Leitrim flavour to their overall sound. Their follow-up album, *Take a Chance,* recorded in 1982, saw the vocal duties in the band handled by Kieran Hanrahan's singer-songwriter brother Mike, who had replaced Tony Callanan. This line-up was to gain enormous popularity both at home and abroad, with their eclectic, exciting and high-energy mixture of virtuoso traditional playing and contemporary country-tinged vocals. Two hit-records in 82/83, *Beautiful Affair* and *Walk Away,* written by Mike Hanrahan, came from their third album for Tara Records, *Light in the Western Sky.* This album featured the multi-talented Australian Steve Cooney on bass, guitar and didgeridoo, introduced the band's mix of traditional and contemporary to a pop audience and helped define, and indeed set, the band's musical course for the rest of the decade. With over ten years of continuous touring, album-making and pushing out the definitions of traditional and folk-rock music, Stockton's Wing are still going strong. With a change of personnel (Kieran Hanrahan left the group in 1990 to form the Temple House Céilí Band) and the release of their 1993 album *The Crooked Rose* (Tara), the band is stripped of its rock-pop elements, layered on during the Eighties, and has returned to its core sound—that of fiddle, flute, banjo, guitar and vocals augmented by keyboards, a move welcomed by fans and critics alike. Like De Danann, Planxty or The Bothy Band, Stockton's Wing have evolved a strong, buoyant style which translates into an immediately identifiable sound. It is a sound, based solidly in the traditional music styles of Clare and Leitrim, that will ensure that this vibrant, creative and hard-working group may well survive into the next decade.

One of the most exciting purely traditional album releases of the Eighties, in that it captures the music in its natural environment, was released by two well-known Clare musicians, concertina player Noel Hill and accordion player Tony MacMahon. Their celebrated Gael-Linn album, *I gCnoc na Graí*, was recorded on an autumn night in 1985 in a pub in Knocknagree on the Cork-Kerry border where the musicians played music for set dancers. Hill and MacMahon played, the dancers raised sparks from the pub's stone floor, and Gael-Linn recorded the whole affair and in so doing succeeded in re-creating the energy-charged atmosphere of the house-dances of old. In the words of Ciarán Carson, who reviewed the album in his essential booklet, *The Pocket Guide to Irish Traditional Music* (Appletree Press): "Why does it still seem a radical concept to record the music in the context in which it is played?..... This record is manifestly about something, we need to be reminded that the music does not exist in a vacuum." It is certainly an album which offers us the opportunity to hear traditional music at its very best being played by two masters who generate an honest energy and ambience which is a million miles away from that which could be generated on any high-tech 24-track commercial studio recording. This, as Ciarán Carson wrote, is indeed "about something." It is the real thing in every sense of the word.

Traditional music in the mid to late Eighties could be viewed from two standpoints. Firstly, there was the world of commercial Irish music with its focus on the promotion of the full-time professional traditional and folk performers such as The Chieftains, Clannad, De Danann, Stockton's Wing, the Sands Family, the Furey Brothers, Christy Moore, Dolores Keane and John Faulkner and Mary Black. Then there was the non-professional world of traditional music, represented by the majority of musicians around the country: the fiddlers, pipers, concertina and accordion players who play for the sheer love and enjoyment of the music. These are the musicians who turn out to compete at the various fleadhs; who gather in pubs up and down the country in informal sessions or who throng the streets of Miltown Malbay in County Clare each July to participate in the annual Willie Clancy Summer School.

At the close of the Eighties, with emigration once again ravaging the population, resulting in a significant reduction of numbers buying traditional albums and attending concerts, two distinct classes of traditional musician had established themselves—the professional and the non-professional. For the professional musician or group, the pressures were the same as those of any rock or pop band. Television and radio exposure and touring became vital for the professionals' continued existence in a highly competitive world of contemporary music. The recording of albums had become essential promotional tools for any band and it was no different for the traditional groups or solo artist, who often competed for the same audience.

These are the pressures faced daily by the older-established bands mentioned above as well as the newer bands and solo artists to emerge as the Eighties came to a close. Artists such as Sharon Shannon, Mary Black and Christy Moore are established Irish folk-superstars in every sense of the word. It is true to state that, with the possible exception of U2, Sharon, Mary and Christy are Ireland's most successful traditional and folk artists of all time. Other full-time professionals such as the Davy Spillane Band, Arcady (featuring ex-De Danann bodhrán and accordion players "Ringo" McDonagh and Jackie Daly and Dublin singer Francis Black), Skylark (featuring Gerry O'Connor on fiddle, the great Len Graham on vocals, Garry Ó Briain on mandocello and keyboards and the wizard of the accordion, Máirtín O'Connor), 4 Men and a Dog, Séamus Begley and Steve Cooney, and Altan (hailed as the traditional group for the Nineties), all compete for the same audience. Then there are the part-time groups, such as the family group Na Casaidigh, Buttons and Bows (made up of brothers Séamus and Manus McGuire on fiddles, Jackie Daly on accordion and Gary Ó Briain on mandocello) and two Cork city-based groups, The Steampacket Co, featuring ace uilleann piper Eoin Ó Riabhaigh and Any Old Time (Matt Cranitch on fiddle, Dave Hennessy on melodeon and the ubiquitous Mick Daly on guitar and vocals). The solo performers, among them the master concertina player Noel Hill, fiddle players Martin Hayes and Kevin Burke, pipers Paddy Keenan and Ronan Browne and accordion players Máirtín O'Connor, Charlie Piggott, Joe Burke and Ann Conroy, continue to take their music to all parts of the globe, primarily to America, to be appreciated and enjoyed in concert-halls, clubs, pubs and informal sessions.

Set-dancing too has seen a huge revival in recent years and with it has come the revival of the céilí band, carrying on the tradition of the legendary céilí bands of the Forties and Fifties. Two of the finest new céilí bands presently moving the dancers' hearts and feet are The Temple House, founded by ex-Stockton's Wing banjo player Kieran Hanrahan, the Galway-based Shaskeen Céilí Band and The Moving Cloud, a Clare band which includes acclaimed accordionist Paul Brock, fiddlers Manus McGuire and Maeve Donnelly, the gifted young flute player Kevin Crawford and Carl Hession on piano.

Current Trends, Directions and Developments

Now, in the early Nineties, Irish traditional music lives and thrives as never before. Though for some observers of current trends it is, to borrow from Dickens, both the best of times and the worst of times. There are those who see the direction the music is taking in the hands of groups like Clannad, Moving Hearts, Stockton's Wing or the Davy Spillane Band as corrupting; detracting from and ultimately debasing the inherent purity, beauty and integrity of traditional music and song in its natural form. One well-known traditional musician has stated that, as we approach the end of this century, we are presiding over the demise of pure traditional music. There are others who see the music as an art form in a state of continual evolution, subject to current cultural influences and ultimately strong and confident enough to grow and adapt itself to outside influences, styles and directions, without corrupting the essence of the music. For the most part, however, there is the view that both camps can live in harmony with each other, in the belief that the music will survive in its purest, most traditional forms and will continue to be played and enjoyed by musicians and listeners alike for generations to come. The truth is that there has never been a time when this country has seen so many fine young traditional

PJ Curtis

musicians and singers, both professional and non-professional, practise their art. The music they play is indeed traditional in every sense, yet how different from that of the eighteenth-century harpist or the post-Famine fiddler! These present-day musicians strive, as did their forebears, to express the inner musical voice which moves them while at the same time responding to the cultural and social values of the day. In this way, Irish traditional music as played by musicians in the year 2000 will, and should, continue to reflect the human condition, the deepest resonances of the soul and the free flight of spirit, creativity and imagination. Music is, after all, an eternally flowing river with may tributaries and diversions. It is also one of the highest expressions and celebrations of life and how it is lived and experienced. That there are so many talented and committed young musicians currently playing Irish traditional music is indeed something to be proud of and something to celebrate.

There has rarely been a time when there have been so many creative, talented and exciting bands, groups and individuals active up and down the country. Some follow the path opened up by the pioneering bands of the Seventies and Eighties such as The Bothy Band, De Danann, Moving Hearts or Stockton's Wing. Others, such as the group Deiseal, confidently forge ahead and explore new-age musical routes, relying on a firm grounding in traditional music forms. Musicians such as the Glackin Brothers from Dublin, the Begley brothers from west Kerry or Martin Hayes from east Clare or John and James Kelly (sons of John Kelly Snr, the famous west Clare fiddler and concertina player) prefer to stay close to their musical roots both at informal sessions and on record. Their approach to recording is as it was for Coleman, Killoran or Gillespie: the music is the language—expressive, rich and powerfully articulate; the instrument is the prime voice. There has never been a time in Ireland when there were so many top-quality recording studios, staffed by highly skilled and talented engineers and producers involved in the making of Irish traditional, folk and folk-rock albums which find their way to all corners of the globe. That too is something to be celebrated.

Several new traditional groups continue to emerge and record. The Clare-based group, Fisher Street, featuring Dermot Lernihan on accordion, brothers John and Séamus McMahon on concertina and flute, respectively, and Noreen O'Donaghue on harp and piano, released their very fine debut album, *Out in the Night* (Mulligan) in late 1991. The Galway group, Dordan, founded by tin whistle virtuoso Mary Bergin with Kathleen Loughnane on harp and Dearbhaill Standún on fiddle and viola, released an intriguing album on the Gael-Linn label combining the grace and delicacy of baroque music with the vigorous attack of Irish traditional music. Vigorous attack peppered with raunchy traditional/Cajun/acoustic rock influences is the stock-in-trade of the northern group, 4 Men and a Dog (featuring Cathal Hayden on fiddle, Gino Lipari on bodhrán and Mick Daly on guitar and vocals), whose debut album in 1992, *Barking Mad* (CBM), launched them to instant folk stardom both at home and abroad. Not for this group the serious performing mien of the purist traditional musician. Here is a group intent on having a good time with their music both on record and on stage, with a repertoire which ranges from bluesy folk chestnuts to Fifties rock n' roll classics, self-penned songs and well-known traditional songs and tunes, all played as if their lives depended on it. This musical attitude won them the exceptional acclaim as Folk Roots 1992 Album of the Year. March 1993 saw the release of their second album, *Shifting Gravel,* produced by Arty McGlynn, which displayed a tighter though more country-rock oriented unit. The album also introduced

Kevin Doherty (replacing Mick Daly), a new singer-songwriter of huge potential. Another northern group to show promise is Deanta, a young quintet who hail from Antrim and Derry. They have been working as a unit since 1985 and have one album to their credit on the Green Linnet label. The summer of 1993 also saw the release of an album *Harmony Hill* (Whirl Records), their second release to date, from the County Sligo group, Dervish, a band who have developed a strong musical identity and show great promise for the future.

Commercial album releases have played, and continued to play, an important role in the promotion of all styles of music. There were many other significant Irish album releases in the second half of the Eighties. Dublin-based Claddagh Records, Gael-Linn, Tara Records and the American-based Shanachie and Green Linnet labels and smaller independent cottage-industry labels such as Homespun, Ossian, GTD and Cló Iar-Chonnachta (Galway) contribute greatly to the growing commercial market by continuing to release Irish traditional music and song in its purest forms. It is said that traditional singing in its purest form is a dying art, a discipline somehow sitting uncomfortably with an audience unable or unwilling to listen to, or appreciate, the human voice, uncluttered, raw and pure. Yet album releases from two excellent traditional singers such as the Clare-based singer, Tim Denehy's *A Winter's Tear* (Cló Iar-Chonnachta), and Áine Uí Cheallaigh's *In Two Minds* (Gael-Linn), finds an enthusiastic audience for both contemporary and traditional themes, delivered in a pure uncompromising "traditional" style of singing. In recent years, newer independent labels have emerged, such as Hummingbird, who release Sharon Shannon, Séamus Begley and Steve Cooney and the Voice Squad and Cross Border Media (CBM) who, as mentioned, have had considerable success with the group 4 Men and a Dog.

As suggested earlier, no one can deny the successes enjoyed over the last three decades by Irish groups in what can be termed the commercial folk or traditional idiom. The Clancy Brothers, The Chieftains, The Dubliners, Paddy Reilly, the Fureys, Planxty, The Bothy Band, Clannad, Enya, Moving Hearts, Stockton's Wing, Davy Spillane, Altan—all have gained varying degrees of international success and acclaim. It is common to hear many of our leading traditional musicians guesting on recordings by major recording stars. Uilleann pipes in particular are in great demand. Paddy Moloney of The Chieftains has appeared on recordings by Mick Jagger, Paul McCartney and Linda Rondstadt. Liam Ó Floinn has guested on albums with the Everly Brothers and Kate Bush, and Davy Spillane, as mentioned above, has turned up on many albums. The uilleann pipes in particular have enjoyed an amazing renaissance. Half a century ago, it looked as if the pipes were destined to become extinct. Due to the early and dedicated work of individuals such as Leo Rowsome, Séamus Ennis, Willie Clancy and Dan Dowd and of organisations such as the Pipers' Club and more recently Na Píobairí Uilleann (The Association of Uilleann Pipers), there are more practitioners, in practically every continent, than could ever have been imagined. Now the uilleann pipes can be heard in informal sessions, on pop and rock records and fronting symphony orchestras. Several Irish pop and rock bands, such as In Tua Nua and Cry Before Dawn, have used uilleann pipes in their line-up. So too does the much talked about New York Irish-American rock group, Black 47.

One negative aspect of the present popularity of the uilleann pipes is the use of the instrument on radio and TV advertising jingles to sell everything from butter and turf briquettes to Irish holidays. The over-use of the instrument in this way (in much the same way that the 5-string bluegrass-banjo is exploited to sell Southern Fried Chicken!) presents it in a jokey manner, an instrument not to be taken too seriously.

As mentioned, another significant development has been the use of traditional music in the classical context. The breakthrough came with composer Shaun Davey's suite for uilleann pipes, *The Brendan Voyage* (Tara Records), played by Liam Ó Floinn and orchestra. Conceived by Davey as an orchestral suite for uilleann pipes, *The Brendan Voyage* is based on the story of Tim Severin's voyage in a leather boat across the north Atlantic following the medieval legend of St Brendan. The natural elements and the sea-creatures encountered by Brendan and Severin are portrayed by the orchestra; the pipes represent the boat on its sometimes wondrous, often perilous sea-voyage. Shaun Davey's union of traditional, contemporary and classical forms of music brought to vivid life the legend of Brendan's voyage and the heroic nature of Severin's achievement.

Shaun Davey's marriage of uilleann pipes and full orchestra was warmly received by fans of traditional and classical music alike. Since then, Davey has seen *The Brendan Voyage* along with his later works *The Pilgrim, Granuaile* and the commissioned symphony, *The Relief of the Siege of Derry,* performed in concert and symphony-halls in the UK, the USA, Canada and Australia. Other works of orchestrated traditional themes have been released and performed, among them Micheál Ó Súilleabháin's *Oileán/Island* (Venture), a three-movement suite played by the Irish Chamber Orchestra with Matt Molloy on flute and Micheál himself on piano. 1991 saw the release of *Island Wedding* (Lunar Records/RTE), a new work in sixteen movements for traditional instruments and orchestra. This original composition came from the pen of the highly talented and well-known County Leitrim fiddle player, Charlie Lennon, again featuring the uilleann pipes of Liam Ó Floinn, the fiddle of Frankie Gavin and the voice of Deirbhile Ní Bhrolcháin.

Another recent example of traditional music wed to orchestral arrangements was premiered at the Irish National Day at Expo 92 in Seville. The work, entitled *The Seville Suite* (Tara Records), was composed by producer/musician Bill Whelan and commissioned by the Department of the Taoiseach to commemorate Ireland's involvement in the Expo held in Spain in the summer of 1992. The Suite's eight movements celebrate the historical links between Ireland and Spain. The music derives its inspiration from the adventures of Red Hugh O'Donnell, Earl of Tirconnell, from his disastrous encounter with the English at Kinsale in 1601 to his subsequent flight to Galicia in Northern Spain and the court of the supportive King Philip. The music draws upon the talents of Davy Spillane, Donal Lunny, Nollaig Casey, Máirtín O'Connor, Mel Mercier, Rodrigo Romani and the RTE Concert Orchestra.

1991 also saw the opening at 63 Merrion Square of the Irish Traditional Music Archive, which will no doubt serve as an invaluable public resource for this key area of historic and contemporary Irish culture. The purpose of the archive, which is co-funded by the Arts Council of Ireland and the Arts Council of Northern Ireland and presided over by archivist and music-historian Nicholas Carolan, is to make accessible the music collections and manuscripts, old and new, of collectors such as Bunting, Petrie, and the great twentieth-century collector and scholar, Breandán Breathnach. One of Breandán's crowning lifetime achievements was his extraordinary work, *Ceol Rince na hÉireann* (Dance Music of Ireland). In the words of Tom Munnelly, song and folklore collector and Chairman of the

Traditional Music Archive, "Breandán Breathnach's three volume collection of tunes set the standard of editorial honesty which continues to be the benchmark by which other compilations are measured." Using an extensive computer data-base to facilitate research, the archive staff endeavour to service all reasonable requests for song and tune texts, supply information on traditional recordings, extend help and back-up services required by research students and deal with general queries on traditional music and song from the public at large. In 1980 the Arts Council of Ireland created the post of Traditional Music Officer to oversee, monitor and develop its policies regarding the fostering, preservation, transmission and performance of Irish traditional music. First to hold the post was Paddy Glackin, the renowned Dublin fiddle player and presenter of *The Pure Drop*, a weekly traditional music showcase on RTE television. The present officer is Dermot McLoughlin, himself a fine fiddle player from County Donegal. Since the start, the officer's role was to determine where the Arts Council most effectively spent money in the best interest of Irish traditional music, to focus on areas neglected through lack of expertise and to advise at top level, to expand areas of education and training in the broad sense and most important of all, to be accessible to musicians and public alike.

While there is a high degree of goodwill expressed towards Irish traditional music in its purer forms, much of it may be more voluble than sincere. The success of the group format over the last twenty years or so has, by and large, replaced unaccompanied music and song in the public perception of what traditional music is. The majority of the 150,000 who bought the James Last Band playing Irish tunes on a 1987 album could not, or would not, be persuaded to purchase albums by The Chieftains, De Danann or even Moving Hearts playing the same tunes. A top-selling traditional album in this country would be only a small percentage of the figures given above for the James Last recording or the extraordinary success of Ireland's best-selling album ever—*A Woman's Heart* (Dara), released in 1992 and including Sharon Shannon, Dolores Keane, Maura O'Connell, Mary and Frances Black and Eleanor McEvoy. It is without doubt far more challenging to listen to a solo fiddler or concertina-player for thirty minutes than to ensemble arrangements of the same music which is more easily assimilated by the listener. While traditional music, particularly in certain areas in the west of Ireland, is a natural part of the social fabric, it can no longer be claimed that in general terms, the music or the musician is at one with the community. Traditional musician Fintan Vallely writes, "The facts are that the majority of musicians reside and work in the cities and live in semi-detached housing estates where no one gives a damn for the music, revering instead Daniel O'Donnell and Coronation Street."

It has been well established that the most important aspect of any traditional music idiom is live performance. Only in the listening to and the playing of the music can it survive and be handed on to the generations to follow. Public performance, whether informal pub and club sessions, concerts, festivals, TV and radio appearances, plays a crucial role in bringing traditional music and song to an audience who otherwise might never be exposed to it except perhaps in pastiche-form radio and TV jingles etc. Whether the music is experienced in a folk club, on a concert stage or on record, it will be evident that the music lives and thrives in a way it never has before. Though much of the euphoria and excitement which the music generated a quarter of a century ago has subsided somewhat, there have never been so many young people, both at home and abroad, playing Irish music, singing Irish traditional songs and dancing Irish traditional dances.

There is, of course, a great deal of work yet to be done regarding the collecting, recording and documenting of the older forms of music, song, story and folklore still extant. To this end there are several committed collectors, such as Ríonach Uí Ógáin in the Gaeltacht (Irish speaking) areas and Tom Munnelly in west Clare, active in the field in different parts of rural Ireland.

While many might mourn the passing of the older, purer forms of traditional music and song, there is now a real passion, vitality, and above all, a pride in the music that will ensure its place among all styles of ethnic and traditional music and other more commercial forms of world music. As we approach the end of the twentieth century, there is no doubt that traditional Irish music, under threat of extinction at mid-century, will survive to be played and enjoyed by future generations of Irish and non-Irish alike.

Discography:

A Selection of Irish Traditional Instrumental, Vocal and Related Recordings

Michael Coleman 1891-1945 (Gael-Linn/Viva Voce CEFCD 161).
From Galway to Dublin—Early Recordings (Rounder 1087).
Séamus Ennis—40 Years of Irish Piping (Free Reed/Green Linnet).
Darach Ó Catháin (Gael-Linn CEF 040).
Ó Riada sa Gaiety/Seán Ó Riada (Gael-Linn CEF 027).
The Clancy Brothers & Tommy Makem—Live in Belfast (CBS).
The Dubliners—Collection (Chyme 31415).
Boil the Breakfast Early/The Chieftains (Claddagh

CC30).

After The Break/Planxty (Tara 3001).

The Bothy Band—Best Of... (Green Linnet GLCD 3001).

De Danann—Best Of... (Shanachi 79147).

Matt Molloy, Tommy Peoples and Paul Brady (Mulligan LUN 017).

Broken Hearted, I'll Wander/Dolores Keane and John Faulkner (Mulligan LUNCD 033).

Stockton's Wing—Collection (Tara CD 4).

The Storm/Moving Hearts (Tara).

Harvest Storm/Altan (Green Linnet GLCD 1117).

In Full Spate/Paddy Glackin (Gael-Linn CEFCD 153).

Oileán/Micheál Ó Súilleabháin (venture CDVE 40).

Meitheal/Séamus Begley & Stephen Cooney (Hummingbird HBCD 0004).

Martin Hayes (Green Linnet GLCD 1127).

Chapter Two

Farewell to Erin—Emigration and Traditional Music

"It is estimated that, in the past ten years, about 500,000 emigrated from Ireland to Britain and the USA. There are 44 million people of Irish descent in the United States."

Address to Emigrant Congress, 1991

"No country in the world, in the history of the world, has endured the haemorrhage which this country endured over a period of a few years, for so many of its sons and daughters."

US President John F Kennedy's public address in Dublin 1963.

The year is 1893, and somewhere in mid-Atlantic yet another emigrant ship ploughs its way to its destination: New York's Ellis Island. On board are Ireland's most plentiful export, the hundreds of near-starving, impoverished emigrants forced to leave their native soil to seek new lives in the New World. In a crowded cabin below decks, an old fiddler plays a slow and soulful lament. It is a sound that will haunt the listeners for as long as they live. Grown men and women shed tears for a land and a people they have left behind and will never set eyes on again.

The spectre of emigration has cast its withering shadow on every generation of Irish men and women since the English conquest under Elizabeth I and the imposition of the Anglican Reformation. It is estimated that more than a million Irish had emigrated prior to the Great Famine of 1845-47. In the decade following the onset of famine, over two million departed these shores, mainly to America and Canada. Over the next sixty years, between 1856 and 1916, a staggering four million Irish men, women and children had taken the boat in search of a better life in distant lands. With the exception of a brief fifteen-year period between 1965 and 1980, this human haemorrhage has continued to bleed Ireland of its brightest and best. The present-day emigration figures of over 500 men and women a week departing our airports and harbours for foreign soil is indeed a depressing reality. Not everybody, however, leaves out of necessity. For many, particularly artists in search of a less rigid cultural climate in which to express their art, "the road out of Ireland" is the only road. The nineteenth-century writer George Moore described Ireland as "a fatal disease, from which it is the plain duty of every Irishman to disassociate himself." Even the great George Bernard Shaw left early, feeling that for any Irishman who wanted to achieve success "...on the higher planes of the cultural professions," his "first business was to get out of Ireland."

"We Are Now 44.3 Million Strong," proclaimed the bold headline in the New York based *Irish America* magazine (July 1992). Underneath, the publisher-editor Niall O'Dowd celebrates the 1990 findings of the US Census, which has reported that Irish Americans now number 44.3 million, a 3.6 million increase over the 1980 census figure of 40.7 million. The new figure represents 17.9 per cent of the total US population.

With the hundreds of thousands of emigrants who

departed these shores since the Famine went the musicians, the singers and musicians, poets and storytellers whose creativity and talents had graced the cultural fabric of Irish life and who would contribute greatly to the growth of American folk and country music and indeed the arts in general. Some were to inhabit the cities of the eastern seaboard, New York, Boston and Philadelphia. Thousands more were to push inland, following work on the railroads which were opening up and crisscrossing the entire west. "There's an Irishman buried under every tie of that railroad," said one old railway worker, thinking of the part the Irish tarriers had played in the building of the Great Atlantic-Pacific Railway which linked the east and west coasts of America. The songs *Paddy on the Railroad* and *Drill, Ye Tarriers, Drill* are only two of those composed and sung by Irishmen working on the the transcontinental railway. Other Irish emigrants had pushed west and south to settle the rich farm lands of the mid-west and the Southern States from the Carolinas to the cattle-ranches and prairies of the Texas Panhandle. Who can say what nameless, wandering Panhandle emigrant minstrel had carried the tune *Bold Felim Brady, the Bard of Armagh* from his home on Irish soil to the Texas prairies and heard the tune set to new words as *The Streets of Laredo?* A good number of other songs can be traced back to Irish roots, among the most popular being *Johnny Has Gone for a Soldier, Whiskey in the Jar, Three Nights Drunk* (Seven Drunken Nights), *I Never Will Marry* and *Rose Connolly.*

In every chapter of American history—social, political and cultural—the Irish have played a major role. But it was in the shaping of the folk-music culture of white America that the Irish, and indeed the Scots, were to contribute most.

Along the majestic Appalachian Mountain range, many fiddle tunes, songs and stories remain to the present day practically unchanged from the day they left their native Irish shores, several from as far back as the mid-1700s. One of the most famous of the southern folk-singers was a Mrs Texas Gladden from Virginia, a member of one of the more remarkable of America's folk-singing families. Some time in the 1950s she recalled her Irish roots to one folklorist. "They tell me that the start of it all was when old Jeems Smith, the head of the family and a fiddler, crossed over the great waters from Ireland to the Virginia colony. He came back up here in these hills and found this salt-lick, where the deer were right numerous, built him a homestead and settled down. We Smiths always liked a big family and a good tune more than money."

This then was the music that was to shape and influence early commercial country and string-band styles. Popular country and hill dances too were mainly of Irish or Scottish descent. In his book, *Folk Songs of North America*, the folklorist Alan Lomax writes, "The American square-dances and hoedowns are a mosaic of figures and steps from Ireland and Scotland. The fiddlers play tunes from Ireland and Scotland, though the hoedown fiddler plays with less polish and tunefulness than his Scots-Irish brothers." Ex-Bothy Band fiddler Kevin Burke recalls playing with an old fiddler from Virginia in the early Seventies and discovering that they had several tunes in common. Richard Nevins of Shanachie Records, New York, cites the old-time fiddle tune *Sally Gooden* (originally recorded by fiddler Eck Robertson in 1922) as being "the oldest Celtic fiddle style preserved anywhere, and most likely unchanged by even a hair from the time it got off the boat." *Sally Gooden* is still played by American fiddlers when called to show off their virtuosity.

One of the first stars of commercial American country music recordings was Charlie Poole, whose banjo-playing father had settled in North Carolina after coming from

Ireland on one of the post-Famine emigrant-ships. One piece Charlie would most certainly have played was *Turkey in the Straw,* a tune made popular by Irishman Dan Emmett, the famous black and white Minstrel. Emmet based the piece on an Irish hornpipe. The tune would also have featured in the repertoire of Joe Walker Sweeney, father of the American 5-string banjo, an Irishman who was a member of the group the Virginia Minstrels. Sweeney popularised the banjo throughout America as well as England and Ireland back in 1844. Strains of the music of the Old Country can still be heard in the music of Bluegrass King Bill Monroe, Ricky Skaggs or current Grammy winner and fiddle virtuoso, Mark O'Connor, who boasts of his Irish ancestry. Their music is the living legacy of the countless and nameless Irish musicians and singers who carried the music as a seed to sow in new and fertile lands.

In the late nineteenth century the Chicago Chief of Police, Corkman Francis O'Neill, adventurer, scholar and flute-player, who was born near Bantry in 1849, founded a thriving Irish Musicians' Society of Pipers, Flautists and Fiddlers. O'Neill's driving passion for collecting tunes, heard or learned from emigrant Irish musicians in Chicago, compelled him in the 1880s and 90s to set about compiling the most comprehensive record of Irish traditional tunes ever committed to paper. O'Neill's extraordinary collection, *The Music of Ireland,* containing 1,850 traditional tunes was published in 1903. A condensed version of the latter, *The Dance Music of Ireland,* was published in 1907. These have become the bible of Irish tunes for traditional musicians down the decades to the present day. So devoted was O'Neill to his vision for Irish music that a job on the Chicago Police Force was guaranteed to any newly arrived Irish emigrant who could whistle, diddle or play a bar of a reel, jig or hornpipe. It is a fact that in the late

1800s the Chicago Police Force was unquestionably the most musical uniformed body of men anywhere!

As the nineteenth century drew to a close Thomas Edison's revolutionary recording machine had been further developed by the Columbia and Victor Recording Companies who had begun issuing the first commercially available recordings on Edison cylinders and flat disc, the latter invented by Emile Berliner in 1887. Many of the great Irish musicians were recorded and listed in the Victor and Columbia record catalogues from the early 1900s. There is, for instance, a spine-tingling recording, taken from a cylinder, made in New York circa 1898 by an uilleann piper, possibly the Kerry-born William (Billy) Hannafin, playing two reels, *The Colliers* and *The Salamanca*. Another uilleann piper, James McAuliffe, recorded a number of cylinders in New York in 1899. Among the pieces recorded by McAuliffe during the late 1800s and early 1900s were *The Minstrel Boy, Miss McLeod's Reel, The Pigeon on the Gate,* and *The Coolin.* Songs and ballads too were being recorded and issued commercially, specifically with the new Irish emigrant in mind. One Irish-American recording star from that period was vaudeville singer Dan Quinn. Born in New York of Irish parents in 1859, Quinn began making cylinders in 1896 and he is reputed to have recorded over 2,500 songs for the Edison Phonograph Company over a five-year period, one of which was the well-known railroad work-song, *Drill, Ye Tarriers, Drill.*

At the turn of the century it was reported that there was more Irish traditional music being played in New York, Boston, Philadelphia or Chicago than there was in Ireland. It was only a matter of time before authentic Irish music was to be recorded on a more regular basis by the growing number of commercial recording companies active in and around New York. Musicologist Barry Taylor's researches reveal that the first commercial recording of Irish traditional music was made on 9 January 1917 by two relatively unknown players, Eddie Herborn on accordion and James Wheeler on banjo. The 500 copies of their Columbia disc sold like hot cakes to emigrants thirsty to hear their native music on this exciting new medium. This event had the effect of ushering in a new chapter in Irish music. By the early Twenties there were a number of small independent record labels, such as Celtic, New Republic and the Emerald labels, active in New York, recording and distributing 78s of genuine Irish traditional music. One of the greatest Irish recording stars of this period was the legendary uilleann piper, Patrick J (Patsy) Touhey. Born in 1865 near Loughrea in County Galway, Touhey emigrated at the age of four with his parents to settle in Boston. By his mid-teens he had established himself as a vaudeville entertainer, a comedian working the variety halls along with the famous hoofer (tap-dancer) George M Cohan, the original Yankee Doodle Dandy.

It was in a music hall in New York's Bowery that Touhey fell under the spell of the "White Piper" from Galway, John Egan. Tuohey's fascination with Egan's set of pipes led him to getting a set of pipes made by the great Philadelphia pipe-maker Billy Taylor, who had died in that city in 1892. In a short time Patsy Touhey had incorporated them into his stage act. By his late teens he was touring the music hall circuit, both as a piper playing for step-dancers and with his partner Charles Burke as a comedy double act. It is, however, as a virtuoso uilleann piper that Touhey is best remembered. This is due to his classic recordings made in New York in the first decades of the 1900s. His early pieces, recorded on cylinder as early as 1901, were made for private collectors. Following the success of the Herborn and Wheeler disc, Patsy Touhey's recordings began to be issued commercially and were enthusiastically received by a fast-growing audience, hungry to purchase and listen to these new musical masters and recording stars on this extraordinary, even magical, new medium in the comfort of their living-rooms. We can still marvel at Touhey's stunning virtuosity as we listen to recordings such as *Miss McLeod's Reel*, *The Flogging Reel* or *Jackson's Jig*, played, as Francis O'Neill wrote, "with a shower of fingers" and recorded in 1919 for the Victor label. Two of these recordings can be heard on the Shanachie album *The Wheels of the World*, released in the Seventies. In the late Eighties Na Píobairí Uilleann (The Pipers' Club) compiled and released a cassette which included the best of Touhey's surviving recordings, *The Piping of Patsy Touhey*. The cassette accompanied a book of the same title by Pat Mitchell and Jackie Small, looking at the life and music of this great Irish-American musician, described as "the genial and unaffected wizard of the Irish Pipes" by Capt. Francis O'Neill, the collector and compiler of Irish music. Patsy Touhey died in New York in 1923, leaving behind an invaluable body of recorded work which, seventy years after his death, continues to both amaze and excite fans of uilleann pipes and piping.

Following Touhey's recordings in the early Twenties came the great classic recordings from the legendary Sligo fiddlers, Michael Coleman and James Morrison, the Donegal fiddler, Hugh Gillespie, and the Leitrim flautist John McKenna. These extraordinary musicians were among scores of other fine musicians recently arrived in America. Their 78 RPM shellac recordings made their way to Ireland and influenced entire generations of traditional musicians. Those early recordings are still held in high esteem by many of today's musicians—especially fiddlers. Coleman was, and remains, the most influential Irish traditional fiddler of the century. His amazing fiddle technique—especially his rolls and triplets—have been copied by literally hundreds of players on both sides of the Atlantic.

Sixty-five years on, his settings and pairings of tunes can still be heard wherever fiddlers gather to play traditional music. The most complete and satisfying collection of Coleman's recordings to be released to date can be found on a double CD set, lovingly and painstakingly compiled by archivist Harry Bradshaw and entitled *Michael Coleman* 1891-1945 (Gael-Linn/Viva Voce CEFCDB161).

Other influential Irish and Irish-American musicians to record in the Twenties included Sligo fiddler Paddy Killoran, fiddler and singer Frank Quinn and JP (Pakie) Dolan, both from County Longford, William J Mullaly, the great concertina player from County Westmeath, and the Chicago pipers Edward Mullaney and Tom Ennis. Like Michael Coleman, Killoran's influence on traditional fiddle playing was immense. He left his native Ballymote in County Sligo in 1922 for New York and immortality as a recording star, starting in 1931 with the small Crown recording label and later with the Decca label (Decca was an English recording company that opened its US label in 1934). Killoran worked and recorded both as a solo artist and with the his Pride of Erin Orchestra. Equally prolific in the Twenties and Thirties was Frank Quinn, whose fiddle and voice were to be heard on over 180 recordings for a number of labels between 1921 and 1936. Other Irish recording stars of the period included piper Patrick Fitzpatrick, accordion player Patrick J Scanlon, and the legendary Flanagan Brothers, Michael (banjo), Joe (accordion), and Louis (guitar), whose original 1920s recording of *My Irish Molly-O* was revived to become a hit all over again in the early Eighties when it was recorded by Maura O'Connell and De Danann. It was suggested by one American music historian that during the Twenties and even the Depression Thirties, there was was not one single Irish household on the East Coast of America which owned a wind-up gramophone who did not possess Michael

Coleman or Flanagan Brothers' records. Other leading Irish-American recording stars of the period include the Boston-based Shamrock Band, led by Dan Sullivan Jr and featuring brothers Michael and Billy Hanafin on fiddle and pipes. O'Sullivan's Shamrock Band recorded over 100 selections, mainly stage-Irish vaudeville skits and routines, during the Twenties and Thirties. Other bands to issue 78s were the Chicago-based Bowen's Irish Orchestra and O'Leary's Irish Minstrels, who played and recorded extensively during the mid to late Twenties. It was, according to musician/musicologist Mick Moloney, who has recently earned a PhD in Philadelphia for his study of traditional music in America, "...the Golden Age of Irish music, in the sense that these exemplars of Irish traditional music got the chance to record and were recording. Suddenly top-quality Irish traditional playing was being heard by more people than ever before." Mention too must be made of Galway musician Peter J Conlon, master of the ten-row melodeon (who was among the first wave of traditional musicians to be recorded in New York in the early 1920s) and the virtuoso accordion player John J Kimmel, of Dutch extraction, whose influence on traditional musicians of the period was immense. Though of Dutch extraction, Kimmel's popularity through the first three decades of this century (he began his recording career in 1904 and continued until 1929) may be gauged by the vast number of recordings of Irish traditional music issued by one of the acknowledged masters of the accordion. His recordings were purchased by Irish and non-Irish alike and achieved wide sales distribution. Indeed, one writer cited Kimmel's 78s as having considerable influence on country and string band musicians in the Appalachian Mountains. Kimmel remains a figure of immense interest to the historian of Irish-American traditional music and particularly to lovers of traditional accordion playing.

As the decades wore on, each ship, and later on each plane, brought wave after wave of new Irish emigrants, ensuring a fresh supply of musical talent for the growing number of Irish bars in the booming American cities. The late Forties saw the release of a number of fine 78s on the independent Copley Boston label from the vastly underestimated accordion player, Joe Derrane, whose parents hailed from Roscommon and the Aran Islands. The Fifties saw the cream of Irish musicians resident in New York, Philadelphia, Boston, San Francisco, St Louis and Chicago. In the late Fifties, three stars of traditional Irish music, accordion-players Paddy O'Brien and Joe Cooley and fiddler Paddy Cronin lived in the same apartment block in the Bronx. Also active in New York were the renowned fiddlers Andy McGann and Paddy Reynolds, who, along with Paddy O'Brien and Jack Coen on flute, were members of the famous New York Céilí Band in the late Fifties. Among the other superb traditional musicians to be found at informal sessions with any of the above were the great Lad O'Beirne, Louis Quinn, John Vesey and Martin Wynne. In Philadelphia, fiddler Eugene O'Donnell began to build a reputation as both player and teacher. So too did Ed Reevy, whose genius extended not only to playing the fiddle but also composing tunes, many of which are now part of the general Irish traditional music repertoire. Indeed, there is hardly a fiddler anywhere playing Irish traditional music who does not include a tune or two composed by the extraordinary Ed Reevy. The influence of musicians such as Coleman, Killoran, Gillespie and Morrison in the Twenties and Thirties and that of Cronin, Cooley and Reevy in the Fifties, Sixties and Seventies can be heard in the music of many of the present-day Irish-American traditional musicians. These include such fine players as fiddle stars Eileen Ivers and the extraordinary Liz Carroll from Chicago, a co-founder of the all-women traditional group, Cherish the Ladies; the fine uilleann piper, Jerry O'Sullivan from New York, the multi-instrumentalist boy-wonder from Philadelphia, Séamus Egan and flute player Joanie Madden, whose father Tom Madden—himself a fine accordionist—emigrated to Boston from south-east Galway in the late Fifties.

Down in New York's Greenwich Village in the early Sixties Pete Seeger (a founder-member of The Weavers), a youthful Bob Dylan and Paul Simon sat enthralled at the feet of three County Tipperary brothers, Tom, Paddy and Liam Clancy and Armagh-man Tommy Makem. With their powerful, earthy voices belting out the ballads of their native soil and their trademark Aran sweaters the Clancys became folk superstars both in America and on this side of the Atlantic. (Bob Dylan was later to declare Liam Clancy both a great folk singer and a major influence.) Their albums on Columbia became essential items in the collection of any follower of folk or traditional music. Following their successes in the Greenwich Village folk-scene, the three brothers from the banks of the Suir and their partner from Keady soon found themselves guesting on the top-rated Ed Sullivan Show, heading the bill first at Carnegie Hall and later at London's Albert Hall. The phenomenal success of the Clancy Brothers and Tommy Makem in America served to inject a much-needed confidence in the burgeoning folk and traditional boom back in Ireland.

This was truly a Golden Age in Irish traditional music— should you happen to be a musician living in New York or possibly London. At home in Ireland, the music had, in the Forties and Fifties, almost gone underground to survive while musicians and fans alike awaited the latest recordings of Irish music from America. The younger musicians were not waiting, however: they were preparing to join their fellow musicians in the capital cities of England and North America.

Britain has always absorbed a great number of Irish emigrants, particularly London, Luton, Birmingham, Manchester and Liverpool. The bleak economic vista of the Forties and Fifties forced many musicians to seek work along with their fellow-Irish men and women in England. For thousands of those emigrants the port city of Liverpool, only hours away across the Irish Sea, remained a prime destination, as it has been for countless Irish since the mid-1800s. Liverpool means ships and docks, and those Merseyside dockyards offered work to many Irish emigrants seeking employment. At some point in the late 1800s, Paul McCartney's and John Lennon's forebears arrived on a Merseyside dock off a Dublin-Liverpool Steamer and settled into the bustling city. Lennon's grandfather Jack was born in Dublin, had then emigrated to America at the turn of the century and worked as a professional singer with the Kentucky Minstrels before returning to live in Liverpool, where John's father Fred Lennon was born.

By the late Fifties, a thriving nucleus of traditional musicians was established there. In 1958 or 1959 the famous Liverpool Céilí Band was started. The original band included Kit Hodge, Seán McNamara, Charlie Lennon (uncle of Maurice Lennon of Stockton's Wing) and Eamon Coyne (fiddle), Pat Finn and Billy Kilgannon (flute) and Peggy Atkins (piano). Over thirty years on, a new generation Liverpool Céilí Band is still playing lively, spirited and vibrant music for set dancers and listeners on both sides of the Irish Sea.

For the majority of Irish seeking work, the men and women from Tory Island, Aran, Donegal, Clare or west Kerry, London was the final destination. Where the masses went, the musicians followed. Indeed, the first céilí band ever, the Tara Céilídh Band (founded by London-Irish pianist Frank Lee), is said to have been formed in the Sarsfield Club in Notting Hill as far back as 1918.

The great west Clare fiddler Bobby Casey moved to London in the late Thirties, where he established himself as one of the driving forces in the London-Irish traditional music scene. Bobby had grown up in a music-rich household and learned his art from his uncle Thady and his father, John Scully Casey, in Annagh, near Miltown Malbay. Bobby Casey was followed to London in the early Fifties by his old friend and neighbour, Willie Clancy, the celebrated uilleann piper from Miltown Malbay, and later by another fine Clare fiddler, Joe Ryan from Inagh. We can only guess what magical music the old friends must have made when they got together after their day's work.

Other musicians too were on the move. The highly respected County Leitrim flute player Roger Sherlock had also moved to London around this time and no doubt found solace in the brotherhood of music shared by musicians of the like of Casey and Clancy or the gifted County Galway accordion player Raymond Roland. Willie Clancy was to return, on the death of his father, Gilbert, to live in his native Miltown Malbay in 1957. The remaining musicians, such as flute player Paddy Taylor, fiddlers Lucy Farr and Jimmy Power (members of the Four Courts Céilí Band), Michael Gorman, Máirtín Byrnes, Danny Meehan and renowned music-teacher and multi-instrumentalist Tommy McCarthy were to become the mainstays of the traditional music scene which thrived in London during the Sixties and Seventies. The celebrated sean-nós singer Joe Heaney also lived in London for many years. He first emigrated to Glasgow in 1947 before moving to London in the Fifties where he performed regularly at the Ewan McColl-AL Lloyd run legendary Singers Club.

The early Sixties saw new waves of emigrants arrive off

the boat and with them came a fresh batch of fine young musicians who would eventually join Bobby Casey, Roger Sherlock and Raymond Roland in the legendary session haunts like the Garryowen, Galtymore, the Shakespeare, the Bedford Arms, the Black Cap, the Laurel Tree, the Fulham Broadway, the Irish Centre in Camden Square and the Irish Club in south London's Eaton Square. One famous London-Irish pub, the Eagle in Camden Town, became so famous a meeting-point that in the Fifties, according to fiddler Brendan Mulkere, "...as many as fifty musicians could be found in the Eagle on a Monday lunchtime. Nobody had any notion of going on to the site, including foremen and gangers!" Brendan Mulkere eloquently articulates the dilemma of the Irishman or woman adrift in the "...most uninviting and uninteresting environment imaginable." "In the pub," Mulkare wrote, "the musician was in a different element: the music was trigger in a mechanism which allowed people who had to work and live in a strained way without the charade of mimicry." With the waves of early-Sixties emigrants were a younger batch of talented musicians. Among these were the great northern fiddler from Armagh, Brendan McGlinchey; John Bowe, an accordion player from County Offaly; the late Kieran Collins, the great tin whistle player from Gort in Galway, and the Clare musicians, fiddler Brendan Mulkere and flute player PJ Crotty. Mulkere, like Tommy McCarthy and Tommy McGuire before him, went on to establish himself as a renowned and tireless music teacher. Today there are countless young fiddlers, pipers and concertina players—Irish, London-Irish and English alike—who owe their highly-developed skills almost entirely to the boundless energies, unselfish dedication, commitment and enormous talents of the great music masters, Tommy McCarthy, Tommy McGuire and Brendan Mulkere. Mulkere also established a small recording label, Inchicronin, which he ran from a tiny room in his London flat. From here he regularly issued albums of Irish traditional music recorded by the cream of the London-Irish musical fraternity. Two of the best-selling Inchicronin albums from that period were *Lord Mayo* and *Arís* by the group Le Chéile, which included PJ Crotty (flute), Danny Meehan (fiddle), Raymond Roland (accordion) and Liam Farrell (banjo). To attend any of the above-mentioned pubs on a weekend night was to witness what amounted to a mini-fleadh in full spate, with the regular musicians locked in musical communion with visiting fiddlers, flute players or pipers.

There was no session without a song or two and in the midst of the fiddles, flutes and concertinas, the powerful voice and banjo of Margaret Barry, accompanied often by fiddler Michael Gorman, would rattle the rafters of pubs, folk-clubs and céilís with songs like *My Lagan Love,* sung as only Margeret could sing it. Both Margeret and Michael became regular performers in the hundreds of folk clubs springing up in the wake of the English folk boom from John o' Groat's to Land's End. From the mid to late Sixties and early Seventies, it was also common to witness a youthful Paul Brady, Mick Moloney, Christy Moore, Eddie and Finbar Furey or Dolores Keane, with her husband John Faulkner, playing and singing in Fulham, Camden Town or any of the other established London-Irish venues, availing of any opportunity to perform their growing repertoires of tunes and songs.

While artists such as Paul Brady, Christy Moore and Dolores Keane had to return to their native land and wait several years for success, the brothers Eddie and Finbar Furey became the darlings of the English booming folk-music and later the rock circuit in the mid to late Sixties. Their gutsy, powerful, soulful playing and singing was a revelation to most of their English listeners, most of whom would have been exposed only to a sedate and mannered folk-music culture. Thirty years on, the Fureys are still playing as a group, and though their music has lost some of its hard edges, the passion and guts evident in the Sixties are still there in abundance.

"They truly were great days," fiddler Brendan McGlinchey recalled in a recent interview with RTE presenter Peter Browne. "You couldn't have heard better Irish traditional music anywhere." With the possible exception of the annual Fleadh Cheoil gatherings, which attracted scores of players from both Britain and the USA, it is a fact that the best Irish music to be heard anywhere was to be heard in English cities with large Irish populations. It was only to be expected, as the cream of Irish traditional musicians and singers now resided abroad, mainly in England, Scotland and North America.

And so it was until the early Seventies, when the outbound haemorrhage was halted as the economy showed signs of recovery. Ireland seemed set on entering a new era of prosperity as many slowly returned from exile to fuel this long-awaited economic upswing. In the Eighties and for the first time since the Famine, a generation of young Irish men and women did not have to face the prospect of emigration as a certainty—as had their older brothers, sisters, aunts or uncles. Now the inbound air-traffic carried the returning Irish and the second and third generation Irish-American visitors anxious to soak up whatever Ireland had to offer. And it had much to offer by way of traditional music and song.

In this fresh dynamic climate of hope, enterprise and economic recovery, Irish traditional music enjoyed a new lease of life and flourished as never before. So much so that a new breed of traditional musician emerged—the professional. Backed by a growing number of indigenous recording companies, a plethora of professional groups and bands emerged. The Dubliners, The Johnstons,

Sweeney's Men, Planxty, The Bothy Band, De Danann, and Clannad packed halls the length and breadth of the country. For a few short years it seemed as if emigration was at an end as both exiled worker and musician returned to their homeland. By the late Seventies, every village in Ireland had its music pubs, where the summer air fairly hummed to the sounds of fiddle, uilleann pipes, flutes, bouzoukis and guitars, entertaining Irish-American, returned exile and native alike, all in search of La Dolce Vita—Irish style, or what became euphemistically termed The Craic.

Any dreams of long-term national prosperity were dashed in the mid-Eighties as a bullish economy began to fail, leaving behind it shattered hopes. Soon the emigrant boats and planes were again crammed with Irish men and women en route to the old shores of opportunity. Once again, traditional musicians and singers were on the move, following the outward-bound human tide. Individuals such as accordion players Joe Burke and Ann Conroy, James Keane and Paddy O'Brien and fiddle-players Kevin Burke and James Kelly, ex-Bothy band members Micheál and Tríona Ní Dhomhnaill, piper Joe McKenna and harpist Antoinette McKenna left to take up residence in America. Traditional bands such as The Chieftains, Stockton's Wing, De Danann, Patrick Street, Arcady and Altan toured frequently, playing to the new emigrants in cities from Boston to San Francisco. The Chieftains, who have been regularly touring the US since their first visits there in the Sixties, have built up a huge following in every state. For thousands of Irish emigrants and second-generation Irish-Americans alike, these frequent concert tours serve as a renewal of the bond which binds the emigrant to their physical and spiritual homeland. Nowadays, each of the great American cities boasts of new, thriving Irish communities and, naturally, Irish pubs to offer the latest arrivals a chance to touch home through social contact with fellow-emigrants and to chase the ever-elusive Craic. Visit one of these pubs on any night of the week and you are sure to hear a fiddler or a flute player, a piper or a singer creating, for a few short hours, a lifeline to a land to which some may never return except on holiday. In essence, what is being created is a home from home, a piece of Ireland.

In the Nineties, groups such as Patrick Street, Arcady and Altan are hugely popular in the States. Altan have won major US awards for their Green Linnet albums *The Red Crow* in 1991 and *Harvest Storm* in 1993. However, they find precious little work in Ireland due to the lack of support from the Irish media who row in behind the more lucrative home markets of rock, pop and country. Ultimately, this is the stark reality: that of fans, and potential fans, who are now to be found in any one of the cities they regularly visit in the US and not in their home towns and villages. One musician declared that it was possible to see more familiar faces at any given venue in the US than it was at an Irish venue at home. Many solo musicians and groups now see Ireland as no more than a rest-up stop between tours abroad. Most see no immediate solution in sight, or at least until there exists in Ireland a real political will and vision to create such an economic climate, that would entice the emigrant home. In the present political climate, however, that possibility seems distant and remote. Indeed, the situation worsens daily with over 300,000 unemployed and the bleak spectre of emigration as the only solution looms for half a million young Irish men and women between now and the turn of the century. Thanks to the Morrison Visa, the "Shores of Amerikay" once again beckon to the thousands of young Irish who seek nothing more than the basic right to work. Unlike their fellow country-men and women of a century ago, their passage from this country will prove less traumatic.

Emigration, like the common cold, seems always to have been with us. Its devastating effects strike at the heart of every aspect of Irish life, social, economic and cultural. The recent emigrants have left behind a country desperately struggling to come of age in the latter decade of the twentieth century, while rising unemployment, business, political and church scandals sweep across the national vista with the relentless, doleful monotony of rain-belts from the Atlantic. The country is further weakened at the loss of our brightest and best to other shores and other cultures. This situation does not augur well for the physical and spiritual health of any nation, least of all for one that has borne the crushing weight of emigration for several centuries.

The year is 1993, and somewhere in mid-Atlantic a sleek Jumbo jet cruises high above the clouds on its way most to New York's Kennedy Airport. On board are Ireland's most plentiful, and valuable, export: a great number of emigrants—young, talented and energetic—off to seek new lives and to join their brothers and sisters on the streets of New York, Boston and Chicago. At the rear of the passenger cabin the late Micho Russell, the well-known whistle player from Doolin in County Clare, en route to play a series of concerts in the United States, plays a slow haunting lament, and the hearts of those within earshot grow sad with longing for a land they will not see for some time, if ever, again. It is reassuring to know that for this latter-day emigrant at least, some things have changed. And as ever, an Irish song or tune, played on a storm-tossed ship in the last century or modern jet plane in this, can serve to comfort the new emigrant, as it did the old. It will remain in the head and heart, a powerful tool for spiritual survival, and as tangible as the hills, the lakes, the rivers, the green grass and very earth of the land from which he or she has departed.

Discography:

A short selection of recordings of Irish traditional music made in the USA and Britain.

USA:

Michael Coleman 1891-1945/Michael Coleman (Gael-Linn CEFD 161).
The Legacy of Michael Coleman (Shanachie 33002).
Classic Recordings of Fiddle Music/Hugh Gillespie (Topic 12T364).
Back in Town/Paddy Killoran (Shanachie 33003).
The Pure Genius of.../James Morrison (Shanachie 33004).
Andy McCann and Paddy Reynolds (Shanachie 29004).
From Galway to Dublin/Various Irish-American, 1920-30s. (Rounder 1087).
The Wheels of the World/Various Irish-American, 1920s) (Shanachie 45001).
An Irish Delight/The Flanagan Brothers (Topic 12T365).
Traditional Music East Coast of America/Various (Rounder RR 6005).
Traditional Music from Chicago/Various (Rounder RR 6006).
Ed Reevy/Ed Reevy (Rounder RR 6008).

BRITAIN:

Paddy in the Smoke/Various—Dance Music In London

Pubs (Topic 12T76).

Memories of Sligo/Roger Sherlock (Inchecronin 7419).

Music of a Champion/Brendan McGlinchey—Fiddle (Silver Spear PSH 100).

The Wind That Shakes the Barley/Jim McKillop—Fiddle (Decca GES 1151).

Her Mantle So Green/Michael Gorman—Fiddle (Topic-12T123).

Arís/Le Chéile (Inchecronin 7423).

Chapter Three

Come Dance with me In Ireland

A Brief Look at Irish Set-Dancing Since the Seventeenth Century

Part One: High Sparks From Stone Floors

"Nobody, unless one has seen and also *felt* it, can conceive the inexplicable exhilaration of the heart which a dance communicates to the peasantry of Ireland."

> Francis O'Neill, author of one of the most famous collections of Irish traditional music, *The Dance Music of Ireland*, published in 1907

"It was unfortunate that in the general scheme to recreate the Irish ballad, the work of our old national dances should have largely fallen to the lot of those who were poorly equipped for the task. For the most part they were lacking in insight, and a due appreciation of the pure, old style, and had, it appears, but a slender knowledge of the old repertoire."

> Francis Roche, *Collection of Irish Airs, Marches and Dance Tunes*, 1927

"...dancing as if language no longer existed because words were no longer necessary."

> Brian Friel, *Dancing at Lughnasa*, 1990

Long, long ago in Ireland, long before Acid-house, the Twist, the Shake, the Jive, the Hucklebuck and long before the One-step, the Foxtrot or the Waltz ever found their way to these shores, several generations of Irish men and women—young and old alike—stepped it out to any one of our own native traditional dances. The Irish loved to dance and did so, it appeared, at every opportunity. Arthur Young, an eighteenth-century traveller in Ireland, wrote, "Dancing is almost universal in every cabin and dancing masters travel through the country from cabin to cabin with a fiddler or blind piper; and the pay is sixpence a quarter." Dancing masters were familiar sights in rural Ireland for several hundred years as they traversed the roads, each commanding his bailiwick, or "patch," of one or more parishes. Their dancing classes were conducted in local houses in winter and outdoors, usually at crossroads, on Sundays and long summer evenings.

The types and styles of dances varied from place to place; in Donegal, Highlands (a variant of the Scottish Highland Fling) were danced, while in Kerry, Slides and Polkas were the order of the day. The most popular dances in Clare and Galway and other counties were the Sets. These included the Plain Set, the Half-Set, the Caladonian, the Lancers, the Orange and Green Set, the Quadrille and more formal dances such as the Walls of Limerick and the Siege of Ennis. The latter dances had evolved from military dances, and indeed the Caladonian and the Quadrille (popular in west and north Clare) also had a military connection, as they are said to have been introduced to western Ireland in the mid-1800s by soldiers returning home from the Napoleonic Wars. (The Quadrille is known to have been danced in Paris, London and Dublin as far back as 1816.) But whatever the dance, they were stepped out to the Jig, Reel, Hornpipe, Slide, Polka or Highland, played by a piper, fiddler, flute player or concertina player.

A musician's worth was estimated by his or her ability to keep good time for the set-dancers. The well-known west Clare musician and member of the Kilfenora Céilí Band, the late Jimmy Ward, recalled, "In my youth, you were strictly judged by the way you played for the set. Nothing else mattered.... There was no such thing as a musician coming into a house and expecting people to sit and listen to him. Your function was to play for the dancers...nothing more." In the absence of an instrumentalist, anybody who could hum or "diddle" a tune was employed to provide the music—"puss music" as it was called. Later, in the Thirties, Forties and Fifties, in the houses that were lucky enough to possess them, the wind-up gramophone was set up in the kitchen, where the dancers could dance to old, well-worn 78 RPM records scratchily blaring from the sound horns of these machines.

So for many generations, Irish men and women looked forward to the hour when they could be free of their labours and gather in local houses for "soirees" or at crossroads and happily dance away to their leisure hours to the music of a travelling piper or fiddler. A comfortable, romantic image, but unfortunately the reality was very different indeed. For three hundred years or so, from the seventeenth to the twentieth century, Irish dancing had been under attack. Not, as one might suspect, from the British authorities and overlords—who considered dancing as a harmless diversion—but from the Irish Catholic Church.

"Dancing," thundered one parish priest in 1670, "is a thing that leads to bad thoughts and evil actions. It is dancing that excites the desires of the body. In the dance are seen frenzy and woe, and with dancing thousands go to the black hell." This indefensible attitude to what was nothing more than a harmless pastime enjoyed against the bleak economic backdrop of pre and post-Famine Ireland was maintained by the clergy right up to the 1930s and 40s. In his excellent essays *The Church and Dancing in Ireland,* the late historian and folklorist, Breandán Breathnach, catalogues what must be considered as nothing short of an unrelenting campaign of terror waged by the clergy against not only dancers and dancing but also any musician who played for such "depraved and sinful" gatherings. Tales of priests breaking up house-dances and open-air dances and condemning the participants to eternal damnation from the altars were legion, the ultimate penalty invoked being excommunication. They went even further; to physically attack musicians and break their instruments, in many cases forcing the player, who depended on his music for his livelihood, into the poorhouse or to take the emigration boat. Stephen Ruane, the nineteenth-century Galway piper, was one such victim, being forced to abandon his living as a professional musician and take to the Galway workhouse, where he ended his days. A Clare fiddler went so far as to argue the point with his local parish priest. The action of the fiddle-bow being drawn across the fiddle-strings, he offered as a defence for playing "the Devil's Music," symbolised the Sign of the Cross and therefore could not be an "instrument of evil." Junior Crehan, the celebrated fiddler and storyteller from west Clare, recalls a priest in his parish in the Thirties who was so vehemently opposed to music and dancing in any form that he regularly prowled the country lanes at night in his efforts to stamp out these "occasions of sin and debauchery." On one occasion, on discovering a dance in full spate in a country house, the over-zealous cleric stormed the house, practically foaming at the mouth, scattering the dancers with his blackthorn stick and snatching a concertina from the hands of a musician, ripping it apart, throwing in on the fire and placing his boot on the instrument while promising Hell, fire and damnation to all who had attended. Such was the genuine fear locally of these threats that the house-dances and crossroad dances died away and many of the musicians emigrated to England or America. "I hung up my fiddle after that," recalls Junior Crehan. "There was no more music to be heard anywhere."

The arrival, in the Twenties, of the modern dances, such as the Waltz, the Foxtrot and the Quick-Step, served only to increase hierarchical blood-pressure. The bishops and priests roundly condemned these imported dances and those of their flocks who were attracted to them. In 1924, the neurotic craze for these new dances was such that the then Bishop of Galway, Dr O'Doherty, declared, "The dances indulged in are not the clean, healthy national dances but importations from the vilest dens of London, Paris and New York." At a Confirmation ceremony in the Galway diocese, the Bishop went further to advise more strict parental control. "Fathers of this parish, if your girls do not obey you, if they are not in at the appointed hour, lay the lash upon their backs. That was the good old system and that should be the system today."

By the Thirties, the clergy, police and state were all in agreement. This whole business of dancing, both traditional and modern, must be brought under control once and for all. This the state did by enacting the Public Dance Halls Act, 1935 (under severe pressure from the Catholic hierarchy), which required all public dances to be licensed and laid down strict conditions under which such licences might be granted. It spelt the end of the homely house-dance and crossroads dance, which were now not only sinful but illegal acts. The clergy, often aided by the police, methodically set about ending these age-old traditions. Parochial halls were built in every village and town to accommodate such public dancing as might be allowed by the local clergy. It caused one musician to reflect some years later: "Traditional music was never the same since they drove it from the fireside."

Traditional music and dancing, however, were not yet whipped into submission. Itinerant dancing masters still held classes, and some of those are still remembered. Junior Crehan recalls with great affection and clarity the two long visits made by the legendary musician and dancing master from west Limerick, Pat Barron, who had been on the road as a music teacher and dancing master since he was sixteen. "I got several tunes from him and when he danced," Junior reminisced, "he was King of the Floor!"

The clergy-controlled hall-dances generated the evolution of the céilí band, basically an extension of the house-group of musicians, whose job it was to attract dancers to the few dances permitted annually. The better the band, the greater the crowd; the greater the crowd, the greater the flow of cash into church coffers. A good céilí band was required to have one principal asset: that was to produce music with such spirit and rhythm that it would "send the dancers' feet through the ceiling." A poor band, lacking such qualities, would cause set-dancers to bemoan, "they would stick you to the floor." Such comments could mean the kiss of death to an aspiring céilí band, as the dancers created their own hierarchy of "craic" céilí bands. Bands which produced extremely spirited and rhythmic dance-music included the Kilfenora Céilí Band, the Tulla Céilí Band (whose heyday bridged the Fifties and Sixties) and the Castle Céilí Band, among others. These were among the bands who guaranteed packed parochial halls the length and breadth of the country.

The Sixties heralded several major changes to the Irish dancing scene. Firstly, the bands began to notice that most of their dancing fans were now to be seen at the London Irish dance venues, as heavy emigration continued to take its toll. The emergence of an indigenous "Beat generation" meant that many young Irish men and women rejected most forms of Irish music and dance. The Twist and the Shake became national dance-crazes. The other factor was the emergence of Seán Ó Riada and and other individual musicians, such as uilleann pipe virtuoso, Séamus Ennis, whose music demanded a listening, almost passive audience. Now there existed two distinct forms of Irish traditional music—music for the head and music for the feet. By the Seventies, with such bands as The Chieftains, Planxty, The Bothy Band and De Danann playing in concert halls and pub music-venues, the sight of a Set or Half-Set being danced was a rarity indeed. Once again, Irish dancing, or "céilí dancing" as it was also called, faded from the public eye; only this time the Church could not be blamed for its demise.

And so the question now is, how is it, in 1992, given all that has gone before, that Irish Dancing, Set-dancing, Céilí dancing, call it what you will, is back with a vengeance? Without the usual fanfares, headlines and hype which attend other dance-crazes, the last few years have seen an extraordinary growth in the number of people from all walks of life who regularly take to the floor for any number of the set-dances being taught and danced in almost every county. Clubs and ad-hoc groups have been formed up and down the country to revive the old dances and also to learn new ones from any one of the several latter-day dancing masters who have emerged. Among the best-known are Joe O'Donovan, Connie Ryan and Timmy "The Brit" McCarthy, who invest an enormous amount of their time and energies in organising weekend dance-workshops and the day-to-day teaching of the finer points of the many set-dances now being revived and being learned by a new generation of extremely keen set-dancers. "Set-dancing from all parts of Ireland is very much alive and practised and our native culture preserved." So wrote Connie Ryan, one of the most commited and energetic of the current dancing masters. "Our music and dance are flourishing as a team effort; and players and dancers are getting the maximum enjoyment, joy and entertainment from it." It would certainly appear that the majority of set-dancing students are now happy to learn to dance for the sheer love and enjoyment of a traditional art form. This is surely a welcome improvement on the situation in the Seventies and Eighties, when the winning of set-dancing competitions seemed to be the main driving factor among the set-dancing fraternity.

Dancing master Joe O'Donovan, in an essay written in 1981 entitled *Traditional Dancing Today*, articulated, as Francis Roche did back in 1927, some of his chief concerns about the dancing scenes of the day. Contemporary dancing, both step and set-dancing, had, he argued, undergone so many changes that "a substantial part of Irish dancing is so far removed from the traditional form that it can no longer be said to be traditional." He asked for a return to the old set-dancing values and had strong words to say about the choreographers of the day who "vied with each other to see which one of them could introduce the greatest number of intricate convolutions, along with the greatest amount of noise." He went on to urge dancers to seek out the old dancers who could "demonstrate and pass on the real tradition." It is almost entirely due to the energy, total commitment and sheer love and understanding of the form by individuals such as Joe O'Donovan and the others, as mentioned, that many of the old set-dances are still extant.

Musician and music teacher, Frank Custy, is one of the people critical of some disturbing trends in present-day set-dancing. "Much of the set-dancing these days is all about speed. It's not good for the music. When you compare the present-day dancers with the old-timers, there's no comparison. The older dancers knew the tunes and this is a great 'lift' to the players. There are many dancers these days who don't know the music and only need a fast rhythm. I don't know why some dancers bother with musicians at all.... Why don't they get a tape recording and stick with that? Thankfully, not all dancers take this approach...but it's not healthy in my opinion."

Paul Brock, the highly respected Clare-based accordion player whose solo album *Mo Chairdín* has recently been released on the Gael-Linn label, co-founded, along with fiddlers Maeve Donnelly and Manus McGuire, The Moving Cloud group specifically to play for set-dancing. He considers dancing to go hand-in-glove with Irish traditional music. "One of the most appealing aspects of set-dancing and indeed playing for set-dancing," Paul says, "is its sociability. Apart from the skill required, set-dancing attracts people from right across the social divide and embraces all age groups. There's a genuine happy and joyous atmosphere created at dances, and more and more people are beginning to recognise that." Paul formed The Moving Cloud to re-capture the feel and drive of the old recorded dance-bands, led by such legends of traditional music as Paddy Killoran and James Morrison. Both Morrison and Michael Coleman, the great fiddler, were in their day also renowned dancing masters. Paul Brock admits to being greatly attracted to the spirit in their music. "There was a rhythm and a lift to their music that must have come from playing for set-dancers. It's a feel The Moving Cloud tries to capture when we play for sets." Witnessing the throngs of energetic set-dancers who attend The Cloud's regular gigs is proof positive that the "rhythm and lift" Paul Brock speaks of have been captured by the band and communicate directly with the dancer on the floor.

The Moving Cloud and the Templehouse Céilí Band (formed by ex-Stockton's Wing member Kieran Hanrahan) are two of the newly-formed bands to attempt to cater almost exclusively to a dancing audience. And more and more, ordinary people are re-discovering the simple delight and enormous pleasure that is to gained from trying their hands (and their feet) at dancing a set, unchanged since their forefathers danced them at "soirees," crossroads and céilís down the years. After generations of persecution, lack of interest, poor image and bad press, it is good to report that Irish set-dancing is alive and well and living not only in Ireland but also in London, Paris, Sydney, New York, Chicago or anywhere a musician strikes up an Irish reel or a jig which touches the spirit and moves the feet. This time, it is hoped, the clergy will be a little more accommodating.

Seán de hÓra, the Clare poet, wrote in the mid-eighteenth century:

"Make and burn warm fires for us.
Fill to us on the table, abundance of wine,
play music for us, the pipe and hautboy,
the sweet golden harp and the hearty fiddle."

No doubt there were Sets or Half-Sets danced at that gathering with the same verve and spark as there would be at a present-day céilí. Thomas Davis once wrote, "To educate is to be free." Thousands of Irish set-dancers the world over would now say, "To dance is to be really free."

Part Two: The Minstrel Boys

Journeys of an Irish Jig

"Oh, I come from Alabama,

with a banjo on my knee."
  Oh, Susanna, Stephen Foster

One of the most popular television shows throughout the
Sixties and the early Seventies was the *Black and White
Minstrel Show,* a weekly visual extravaganza which was
watched by hundreds of thousands of viewers in England,
Scotland, Ireland and Wales. The show had enormous
appeal, with its blacked-face, all-singing, all-dancing
minstrels, decked out in top hats, tails and white gloves
and lines of beautiful high-kicking dancing girls.
Ultimately, because of pressure from groups that brought
the Race Relations Act to bear on the BBC, the show was
axed to the utter dismay, no doubt, of its countless fans. In
the political climate of the Seventies, the image of the
white artist-entertainer blacking up to croon *Way Down
Upon de Swanee Ribber* or *Massa's in de Cold, Cold
Ground,* had become deeply offensive to both blacks and
whites fighting for better race relations.

The tradition of white singers and dancers "blacking
up" goes back to around 1750 when an itinerant troupe of
actors and musicians called "The Ethiopian Deliniators"
were shipped in to Kentucky from the Caribbean to
entertain the elite and well-to-do of that state. This group
of performers were neither Ethiopian nor African nor
indeed European. They were, in fact, Irish migrants, just off
the boat and desperate to make a living. They did so by
blacking their faces, strumming banjos, an instrument
hitherto unknown in the New World, and dancing a step-
dance that was a hybrid of an African foot-stomp and an
Irish jig. And so the black-faced minstrel was born and,
from 1750 on, the Irish were to dominate the the tradition
right up to the early part of this century.

"The Irish simply blacked-up," writes the black scholar
and playwright, Leni Sloan, "disguised themselves as Afro-

Americans and became one of the first generations of American minstrels. They created one of the real cornerstones of the American stage." The legacy of minstrelsy lingered well into the twentieth century—two of the most famous balck-faced minstrels being the great Al Jolson and Bert Williams. *Billboard,* the American showbiz magazine, published a "minstrelsy" column regularly until 1939 and many minstrel songs found their way into the repertoires of early country singers. Some country singers, such as Jimmy Rogers and Roy Acuff, had worked as black-faced minstrels in their youth. In his excellent book, *Country,* Nick Toches cites The Rolling Stones as being an example of latter-day minstrelsy. He writes, "It was minstrelsy without black-face, but minstrelsy just the same."

The history of minstrelsy in America is peppered with great names, all of them Irish or Irish-American—TD Rice, Dan Emmet, George Christy and Bill Witlock, to name but a few. Other Irish-Americans who started their careers as minstrels went on to become the great names in American tap-dancing, or "Hoofers," as they were termed: Pat Rooney, Eddie Horan, Barney Fagan, George Primrose and the greatest of them all, the original "Yankee Doodle Dandy," George M Cohan. (Galway-born Patrick, "Patsy" Tuohy, comedian and virtuoso uilleann piper, worked the vaudeville circuit with Cohan for several years.) The great nineteenth-century American songwriter, Stephen Foster, whose great-grandfather Alexander Foster had emigrated from Derry around 1728, started his songwriting career in Kentucky by writing for travelling minstrel shows. His songs such as *My Old Kentucky Home* and *Old Black Joe* went on to become a large part of the staple popular music diet of America, particularly in the Southern states. One of his songs, *Hard Times,* was revived by Mary Black and De Danann in 1984. Foster's best-known song of the period, *Oh, Susanna,* became a classic minstrel song, originally made famous by the Christy Minstrels around 1850, and it survived to become the most-requested piece on the *Black and White Minstrel Show* in the Sixties.

Minstrelsy's first true star was Thomas Dartmouth or "TD" Rice (1808-1860) who developed the Ragtime image of the minstrel as both con-man and dandy—the archetypal black-faced minstrel. Rice introduced a new dance into his popular routine called the "Jim Crow" or "Jump Jim Crow," which he married to an old Irish fiddle tune. From this dance came the "Buck and Wing" and the "soft shoe shuffle" much favoured by the famous "hoofers" of the early twentieth century. It's said that Rice had come on the idea for the dance after seeing a young black slave boy dancing his version of an Irish jig in a back alley next to where Rice was, none too successfully, performing. In his scholarly work, *Songsters and Saints* (Cambridge), musicologist and black music historian Paul Oliver writes: "...there were many black dancers on whom the white minstrels modelled their steps. They drew upon Scots and Irish sources too, and it is still arguable how much the "Ethiopian Jigs" were derived from the Irish jigs, with their rapid footwork and almost motionless upper body and arms."

Afro-Americans had been dancing this strange mixture of Irish and African since they had worked side-by-side with the Irish from as early as 1650, when over 40,000 Irish men and women were deported or exiled from Ireland to work the tobacco plantations in the Caribbean and the southern states.

Bob Callahan, the Irish-American poet and writer, presents an intriguing image of a hybrid culture of music and dance evolving from a century of African and Irish working side by side on the plantation fields. He writes, "You got Ibo men playing bodhráns and fiddles and Kerrymen playing jubi drums. You got set-dances becoming syncopated to African rhythms and so your basic céilí turned into a full-blown voodoo ritual." The "Jim Crow" or "Jump Jim Crow" was one of these dances, and it was one of the dance routines which was to make a name for TD Rice in the 1840s.

After Rice came black-face minstrel/writer/singer/dancer /musician, Daniel Decatur Emmet and George Christy, who organised troupes of minstrels and entire shows out of Afro-Irish dances, songs and skits. Dan Emmet, by the way, was the man who wrote *Dixie, Old Dan Tucker* and *The Blue-Tailed Fly (Jim Cracked Corn),* the melody for which he borrowed from an Irish hornpipe. Both songs were absorbed into the American folk song repertoire, the latter becoming a Top Ten hit for Burl Ives in the Fifties. Emmet is also credited as the originator of the piece, *Turkey in the Straw,* probably one of the best-known and most-recorded dance tunes in the history of American country music. The tune appeared in Emmet's minstrel show as *Old Zip Coon* and is said to have derived from yet another Irish hornpipe. The Christy Minstrels and Emmet's Virginians paved the way for the hundreds of professional black-faced minstrel troupes—the Kentucky Minstrels, which, in an early 1900s manifestation of the group, had among its numbers one Jack Lennon, born in Dublin and grandfather to Beatle, John Lennon—the Congo Melodists and the Ring and Parker Minstrels. These exotic troupes, made up almost entirely of Irishmen, travelled both north and south of the post-Civil War Mason-Dixon line to dance, sing and clown their way into the history books while creating one of the most fascinating and vibrant American art forms of the time.

Dan Emmett's Minstrels, a.k.a. The Virginia Minstrels, landed a six-week engagement in London in 1843. Among his troupe were banjo-playing Irishmen Billy Whitlock and Joe Sweeney of Appomatox, Virginia. Sweeney was the man credited with popularising the 5-string banjo in America, where it found its way into "old-timey" mountain music, New Orleans jazz and Bluegrass. The banjo had originated in Africa as a lute-like instrument, called a "banjer," and had come with the slave ships to the tobacco and cotton plantations of the West Indies and the southern states. Sweeney and the Virginia Minstrels are also credited with introducing the banjo to Ireland in 1844, where the 4-string tenor banjo was later adopted to play Irish music. (Present-day virtuoso practitioners include Barney McKenna of The Dubliners, Kieran Hanrahan, Davey Arthur of the Furey Brothers, Mick Moloney, Kevin Griffin and Gerry O'Connor.) Another of these minstrel troupes, the Serenaders, also travelled to England in the mid-1800s and performed at Buckingham Palace. We can only guess what the Palace inmates made of these black-faced minstrels with Afro-Irish accents. Perhaps it was the legacy of the Serenaders which urged George Mitchell to create his "Black and White Minstrels" who went on to television fame and fortune in the Sixties.

If you ever have the good fortune to visit New Orleans, do try and visit Jackson Square on any Sunday morning. There you will witness the essence of the rich New Orleans culture of music and dance. Jazz bands, blues and gospel singers abound. So too do the solo dancers. And as you watch the dazzling footwork of the amazing young black tap-dancers step it out for quarters and dimes, just remember you are watching the descendant of the Irish jig or hornpipe, having left these shores as far back as the seventeenth century to step-dance its way from Irish kitchens and crossroads onto the coffin-ships to the tobacco-plantations of the Caribbean or the Virginias; on to the Minstrel shows and the American and English music halls, and finally into the homes of millions on the television screen in the 1960s.

Perhaps one day, a comprehensive study will be carried out on the long, complex and extremely fascinating journeying of some Irish and African traditional dances and the Irish and Irish-American black-faced Minstrel Boys who danced them.

Discography:

Set Dancing Tapes Vols 1-6 (NPU 002—NPU 007).
Available from Na Píobairí Uilleann, 15 Henrietta Street, Dublin 1. Phone 8730093.

PART TWO

THE MUSICIANS
Profiles of Clare musicians, past and present

"We are the music-makers,
And we are the dreamers of dreams,
Wandering by the lone sea-breakers,
And sitting by desolate streams;
World-losers and world-forsakers,
On whom the pale moon gleams:
Yet we are the movers and shakers
Of the world for ever, it seems."

From *Ode* by Arthur O'Shaughnessy (1844-81).

Patrick J "Patsy" Tuohey with his wife, Mae.
(Courtesy of Na Píobairí Uilleann)

Johnny Doran (at right) with Pat Cash and Cash's son, Michael, at the Green Lanes, Walkinstown, Dublin, in the early Forties.
(Courtesy of Na Píobairí Uilleann)

The Kilfenora Céilí Band
Back Row (L-R): Gerry Lynch (accordion), Paddy Mullins (flute),
Gerald O'Loughlin (drums), Jim McCormick (flute) and Pat Madigan
(saxophone). Front Row (L-R): PJ Lynch (fiddle), Tom Eustace
(fiddle), Gus Tierney (fiddle) and Kitty Linnane (piano).
(Courtesy of Gerard Linnane)

The Chieftains
(L-R): Kevin Conniffe (bodhrán), Matt Molloy (flute), Paddy
Moloney (uilleann pipes) and Seán Keane (fiddle).
(Courtesy of Claddagh Records)

The Dubliners
(L-R): Barney McKenna (banjo), John Sheehan (fiddle),
Ronnie Drew (vocals/guitar) and Luke Kelly (vocals/banjo).
(Courtesy of Manfred Gierig)

The Bothy Band
(L-R): Paddy Keenan (uilleann pipes), Matt Molloy (flute),
Kevin Burke (fiddle), Tríona Ní Dhomhnaill (vocals/clarinet),
Donal Lunny (bouzouki) and Micheál Ó Domhnaill
(vocals/clarinet).
(Courtesy of PJ Curtis)

Willie Clancy
(Courtesy of Mal Whyte)

Séamus Ennis
(Courtesy of Na Píobairí Uilleann)

Tommy Peoples
*(Courtesy of
Tommy Peoples)*

Seán Tyrrell
(Courtesy of John P Coyle)

Micho Russell
(Courtesy of Tony C Kearns)

Tony Linnane
*(Courtesy of
Tony Linnane)*

Noel Hill
*(Courtesy of
Tony C Kearns)*

Mary McNamara
*(Courtesy of
Mary McNamara)*

Frank Custy
(Courtesy of Catherine Custy)

Paul Brock
(Couresty of Paul Brock)

Sharon Shannon
(Courtesy of Eamon Donovan)

Chapter Four

Tommy Peoples—Master Traditional Fiddler

"Music so forest wild
and piercing sweet, would bring
Silence on blackbirds singing
Their best in the ear of Spring."
        The Others—Séamus O'Sullivan, 1879–1958.

Some months ago, I took an American friend to a well-known north Clare pub to enjoy a good night of traditional music. As we settled in to the session, black pints in front of us, my friend inquired about the identity of the dark-haired fiddle player seated in a corner among a group of other musicians. When I told him who it was we were listening to, a look of disbelief spread across my friend's face.

"That's Tommy Peoples!" he exclaimed. "*The* Tommy Peoples?"

He could not believe that a musician he considered to be a master, a virtuoso fiddle player of world class and international renown, could actually be heard in a local pub. To my friend's utter amazement, and delight, here was a musician of the stature of a Stephane Grappelli or a Yuhudi Menuhin, playing his music, without much of the pomp and circumstance which would surround musicians of similar standing in America or elsewhere. My American friend could also not believe that such a great musician as Tommy Peoples should have to play his magical music to, what appeared to him, a generally uninterested and inattentive audience. As we watched and listened, against the usual backdrop of animated pub chat and laughter, we both concluded that fame—Irish style—is a strange phenomenon indeed.

There are few traditional fiddle players who are more respected or as widely acclaimed as is Tommy Peoples. His fiddle playing on record with the legendary Bothy Band, on his own solo albums, and his "live" performances, indicate musicianship of the highest calibre. His style is unique and individual. It is also unmistakable. No other fiddler sounds quite like Tommy Peoples; though his influence can be detected in the playing of many younger players. It's a style that embraces absolute technical skill and mastery, fuelled by Tommy's own inventive genius and delivered with great feeling and soul. His fiddle playing on tunes like the reel, *The Oak Tree* or the strathspey, *The Laird of Drumblair* or *The Salamanca* (included on the album *The Bothy Band–1975)* demonstrate his extraordinary prowess as a fiddle player, regardless of musical genre. It's probably close to the truth to claim that no other traditional fiddler since Michael Coleman or James Morrison has had the same influence as does Tommy Peoples. One well-known Dublin fiddler, now in his thirties, holds Tommy in the very highest esteem: "Tommy is the greatest traditional fiddler ever...for me, he's Elvis and The Beatles rolled into one, in terms of the effect he had on me when I was starting out to play fiddle. There is really nobody like him...he has magic hands." There are countless other fiddlers around the country who hold Tommy in the same regard and who continuously marvel at those magic hands.

Tommy Peoples, now in his forties, was born in St Johnston, County Donegal, a small town on the border with Northern Ireland, and first learned the rudiments of traditional fiddle playing from his cousin, Joe Cassidy. In a county that boasted of fiddle players in every other household, it was no surprise that Tommy soon developed his playing and soaked up the tunes and influences of the area. Since the last century, cultural links with Scotland had shaped local fiddle styles into a unique and exciting blend of Scots-Irish styles. Seasonal emigrants to Scotland to find work as potato pickers usually returned to Donegal with new songs, tunes and dances. This blending of Irish and Scottish music can be heard in the playing of the great travelling fiddle player from Glenties, Johnny Doherty, and the late Frank Cassidy from Teelin. It was in this fertile musical ground that Tommy Peoples developed his playing. By his late teens, Tommy's fiddle style was fully honed and formed. His bowing, his smooth and effortless fingering, his note-decoration and above all his depth of feel for the tunes, placed him in a league of his own.

The early Seventies found Tommy moved from one musical stronghold to another this time to Kilfenora in County Clare, where Tommy married Marie Linnane, daughter of Kitty Linnane, pianist with the famous Kilfenora Céilí Band. He soon became a member of the band and recorded an album with them in the late Sixties. His fame as a traditional fiddle player at this point had spread far and wide. His informal sessions in Dublin in the Sixties with other fine players, such as Matt Molloy on flute and Paddy Keenan or Liam Ó Floinn on uilleann pipes, became the stuff of myth and legend. Matt Molloy was to join Tommy later in The Bothy Band before moving on to become a prominent member of The Chieftains; Liam Ó Floinn went on to join Planxty.

1975 saw the birth of the pioneering band that is now

hailed as one of the most exciting, innovative ensembles ever to play Irish traditional music—The Bothy Band, originally called Seachtar and including accordion maestro, Tony MacMahon.

Prior to this, Tommy had been a member of the short-lived 1691, a band that was better known in Brittany than at home and that featured Tríona Ní Dhomhnaill, piper Peter Browne, Matt Molloy and Dublin singer Liam Weldon. This line-up recorded and released but one album for the Breton Arfolk label. The album had a raw energy and directness and offered a tantalising glimpse of the musical forces which were about to be unleashed. The Bothy Band's original line-up included Matt Molloy, Paddy Keenan, Paddy Glackin, Micheál and Tríona Ní Dhomhnaill and Donal Lunny. Before the band went professional in November 1975, fiddler Paddy Glackin left, to be replaced by Tommy Peoples, and it is Tommy's stunning fiddle work that can be heard on The Bothy's debut album on the Mulligan label, *The Bothy Band–1975* (Green Linnet in the USA). His playing on the track entitled *Hector the Hero* and *The Laird of Drumblaire* is spellbinding.

By now, his status as a fiddle player with few peers was secure. His playing within the group, alongside his old session pal and ex-1691 member Matt Molloy and uilleann pipe wizard Paddy Keenan and coupled to the powerhouse accompaniment of Donal Lunny and Micheál and Tríona Ní Dhomhnaill, created some of the most dynamic, exciting acoustic instrumental music ever produced. It was music that moved artists such as Bob Dylan, Paul Simon and Emmylou Harris to seek out their albums and marvel at the band's instrumental firepower and declare themselves firm fans of the group. Prior to the band's first live concert in London in November 1975, they were being described in the English music press as "legendary." In the words of the English *Melody Maker* critic Colin Irwin, The Bothy Band were, "...instantly lethal." You knew instinctively and immediately that here was a band on another planet from all the others. Their music snarled and exploded in a way no folk band had ever done before. No Irish album goes anywhere near to capturing that exploding musical energy as does The Bothy Band's 1975 debut album. Tommy Peoples' electrifying fiddle is very much a part of that lethal mix.

Life on the road for any professional touring band, folk or rock, is physically, mentally and emotionally demanding. For any well-known folk or acoustic band, (and in particular The Bothy Band at the height of their fame), it often means an unrelenting cycle of travelling across Europe, America and Canada, concerts, television and radio appearances, rehearsing and recording and, invariably, the pressures and temptations to engage in the endless energy-sapping impromptu after-hours music sessions which might follow an equally energy-sapping concert performance. After a year of hectic road work, and scores of unforgettable live appearances in Ireland, Britain and Europe, Tommy and The Bothy Band parted company, with Kevin Burke stepping in as the band's fiddler. Kevin remained with the band until their break-up in 1979.

On leaving The Bothy Band in 1976, Tommy returned to settle in County Clare. During this period he recorded an album for the New York label, Shanachie, entitled *The High Part of the Road*. On that album (the sleeve notes describe him rightly as "...probably the most influential Irish fiddler living today") he is joined by Paul Brady on guitar and offers the listener just a selection of some of the great tunes on which Tommy put his indelible stamp. The reel *The Oak Tree* is pure Tommy Peoples. So too are *The Wheels of the World*, *The Nine Points of Roguery* and *Dinny Delaney's*, on which Tommy employs all his skills and tricks—double-stopping, bent notes, grace-notes and cranning (a technique usually confined to pipes) to tease every nuance and delicate shade from these oft-played tunes.

In 1978 an album simply entitled *Matt Molloy-Paul Brady-Tommy Peoples* was released on the Mulligan label to loud critical acclaim. Tommy and Matt's playing mettle as a duo had been tried and tested many times as session players in the Sixties and as Bothy Band members. Now, with Paul Brady's driving guitar accompaniment, they play up a veritable storm on vinyl, capturing the fierce energy and passion of a live session at its apogee. The album stands as a tour de force, capturing, as it does, the very essence of the music and the spirit of the period, and remains to this day a fitting testimony to the talents of three master traditional musicians.

These days, Tommy confines his playing to the occasional concert appearance and a regular weekly session in a homely Kilfenora pub. Here he can be seen and heard alongside his daughter, Siobhán, who is herself an excellent traditional fiddle player who carries much of Tommy's genius and whose reputation grows with the passing of each day. Tommy's fiddle-playing remains as electrifying and vibrant as ever. Here we witness a musician who explores the very essence of his music, which is the hallmark of the consummate artist. It is music which can elevate even the most downtrodden spirit. His music is also a music which can be stark, bleak and disturbing, often played as if the player is in an intensely personal conversation with a darker, deeper "self." For a musician to venture this deep inside the heart of any music, be it traditional, blues, jazz or classical, not only demands great technical abilities but also takes courage of spirit and soul.

As a musician, Tommy Peoples possesses all these

attributes. His talents can be best summed up by quoting from a short piece written on Tommy by Shanachie label boss, Richard Nevins: "Raw power and poignant emotion are at the heart of Tommy Peoples' music—he fiddles masterfully, bending, twisting, shaking each note for all its expressive worth. He plays as he lives, with fierce need, with disconcerting tenderness and frailty, with reckless, impassioned abandon." It is this desperately provocative tandem of aggression and love that distinguishes his fiddling, that gives rise to its haunting sensuality. What establishes Tommy as one of our greatest fiddlers are the qualities mentioned above coupled with a stunning technical dexterity and authority rarely witnessed since Coleman. Imitators are numerous, but there is only one Tommy Peoples.

Should you have the good fortune to witness Tommy Peoples play his fiddle in a smoky north Clare pub session, you might be forced to marvel, as did my American friend, at how casually we here in Ireland take our master musicians. Yet how important they are to our culture, for they speak a language which embodies and reflects our collective souls. This is the language that Tommy Peoples so eloquently speaks through his magic hands and his fiddle, with sublime mastery and artistry, even as he sits on a concert stage or in a darkened corner of a Clare pub and plays for those who have ear to listen and heart to understand.

Discography:

Tommy Peoples/Tommy Peoples (Comhaltas CL 13).
The High Part of the Road/Tommy Peoples and Paul Brady (Shanachai 29003).

The Iron Man/Tommy Peoples and Dáithí Sproule (Shanachai 79004).

The Bothy Band–1975/The Bothy Band (Mulligan LUN 002/Green Linnet SIF 3011).

Matt Molloy, Tommy Peoples and Paul Brady/Matt Molloy, Tommy Peoples and Paul Brady (Mulligan LUN 17).

The Sound of Stone/Various artists (BAG CD 001).

Chapter Five

Willie Clancy—The Minstrel from Clare

"And he heard it, high up in the air, a Piper piping
away.
And never was piping so sad and never was piping so
gay."

The Host of the Air—WB Yeats

"He began caressing the drones and chanter
and luring them into the feeling
that came over him.
Their steady humming came to us
as he poured out the rebirth
of a wailing cry
that was a piper's lament."

Willie Clancy—Paddy O'Brien

On the rugged, Atlantic-lashed west coast of Clare lies the
quite, peaceful market-town of Miltown Malbay. For fifty-
one weeks of the year the town goes about its daily
business, catering for the everyday needs of the
surrounding farming and rural community and the
increasing summer tourist trade. For one week in early
July, however, the town is awash with activity and comes
alive to the sound of fiddles, flutes, concertinas,
accordions, singers and dancers and particularly uilleann

pipes. And in every pub, back room and street corner at any hour of the day or night for seven non-stop music-filled days, any combination of the above can be heard in full flight, celebrating the memory of Miltown Malbay's legendary uilleann piper, whistle player, flute player and singer, the late Willie Clancy. Since his untimely death in 1973, Miltown has played host to an annual Willie Clancy Summer School, dedicated to the memory of the man and his music.

It has, over the years, become one of the most important, not-to-be-missed events in the cultural calender which attracts musicians and lovers of Irish traditional music from all parts of the globe. Cast an ear on any session and you are likely to hear the players sport Australian, American, Canadian or English accents, though the music they play is 100 per cent traditional Irish. A few years back, a piper from Tibet was seen taking his place amongst a group of Irish players to try his hand at a selection of Irish reels or jigs. Ask any member of The Chieftains, De Danann, Altan, Stockton's Wing or indeed any traditional musician the length and breadth of the country where they intend to be on the first week of July and the answer will invariably be the same: in Miltown Malbay for the Willie Clancy Summer School—the "Willie Week," as it is now affectionately called. And come they do; to teach, argue and discuss, to meet and talk to old friends and to join in musical communion with their fellow pipers, fiddlers and other musicians who regularly attend, making this week one of the most exciting, special seven days in the Irish music calender.

Willie Clancy was a man of exceptional talents—whistle player, flute player, singer, philosopher, story-teller and wit. Above all, he was an absolute master of that most complex and exciting of wind-instruments—the uilleann (elbow) pipes. To have heard Willie Clancy play dance tunes with great spirit and grace or sad, haunting slow airs in the back room of Friel's Pub in Miltown was an experience never to be forgotten. He was in every sense a folk-poet of gigantic stature. Willie was also an exceptional human being—humble, open, friendly and at all times fairly bubbling over with kindness, wit and earthy humour. Anecdotes about Willie's infectious wit abound. Even on the evenings when he would not be in the mood to bring his pipes or whistle to the pub, Willie's razor-sharp humour kept his listeners in high spirits for many an hour. There's a story told of a particular American folklorist interviewing Willie at length about his life and music. The folklorist's general approach and attitude seemingly rubbed Willie up the wrong way, and Willie let him know it in his own inimitable way. "Is there a history of piping in your family?" drawled the irritating folklorist. "There is," Willie snapped. "My mother was a plumber!" The interview ended there. There are few, if any, other accounts of Willie being discourteous or unwelcoming to a soul. He had time for everybody and the gift of making you feel special in his company. His memory for names and faces was impressive, even of those whom he may have encountered only fleetingly, years before. But it was Willie's uilleann piping which endeared him to the thousands who have had the good fortune to hear him either on record or in the flesh. His music, as the legendary Kilmaley multi-instrumentalist Peadar O'Loughlin claimed, "was for the head and not for dancing." Willie Clancy was, in the words of piper and writer Pat Mitchell, who himself fell under the spell of Willie's piping, "a man who embodied everything that was good and noble and generous in the old Irish traditions."

Born on Christmas Eve, 1918, Willie grew up in an atmosphere of music, story and song. Both his mother, Ellen, and his father, Gilbert Clancy, were musicians.

Gilbert had in his youth soaked up the music of the legendary Clare piper Garrett Barry, and by the time Willie reached his teens (he started to learn the whistle at the age of five) his flute playing reflected the influence of Barry's nineteenth-century piping style, passed on to him by his father, Gilbert. Both Bobby Casey and the late John Kelly, who played with Willie around Miltown in the Thirties and Forties, remember Willie as "a great flute player...a natural musician." Willie's first real contact with the uilleann pipes came on hearing the great travelling piper Johnny Doran, who traversed the highways and byways; playing at wakes, weddings, crossroad dances and fairs. The uilleann pipes, which had enjoyed huge popularity in pre-Famine Clare, had become in the early part of this century an almost extinct species. The sight of Johnny Doran playing his pipes on the streets of many villages in the Thirties and Forties must have presented as alien a sight as if he were an Indian sitar or Sudanese ud player.

It is not difficult to imagine how a young and gifted musician such as Willie Clancy would be utterly fascinated and would succumb to the web of magical sound being spun by Johnny Doran and his pipes. Willie was a lively, highly intelligent seventeen-year-old when he first encountered Johnny Doran and his pipes in 1936. So besotted was he with the instrument and its potential he is reported to have followed Doran around the county—to fairs and dances—soaking up his tunes and piping style. His next step was to get hold of a practice set of pipes (a basic bag, bellows and chanter), which he did in 1938 with the aid of Johnny Doran's piping brother, Felix. By the early Forties Willie had mastered the basic piping techniques and by 1947, now playing a full set with drones and regulators, he won first prize at the Oireachtas uilleann piping competition. A private recording made around this time by Paddy Hill (Noel Hill's uncle) shows Willie's musical debt to his mentor and friend, Johnny Doran. Willie's setting of the Doran showpiece reel, *Rakish Paddy*, clearly demonstrates this, while at the same time it gives us a look at the early stages of what was to become a highly distinctive and individual style of piping. Willie was also much influenced by local west Clare styles, especially the fiddle playing of Scully Casey (father of the great fiddler Bobby Casey), and incorporated much of Scully's ornamentation into his flute playing and later his piping.

Being an exceptional piper in the west of Ireland in the late Forties or early Fifties did not put "shoes on the feet or food on the table," and so Willie was forced, like many of his contemporaries, to emigrate to London, where he found work as a carpenter. Prior to moving to London, Willie spent some time in Dublin, where he came in contact with many fine musicians, including some of the great Dublin pipers, among them John Potts, Séamus Ennis and Tommy Reck. These pipers were of the tight fingering school of piping, and Willie blended this technique into his own legato style, to evolve what is now referred to as the Clancy style of piping.

With the death of his father in 1957, he returned home to Miltown Malbay, where he lived, worked, played his music and sang his songs until his own death in 1973. By the early Sixties, Willie had evolved a piping style that was to win him countless devotees; among them were future uilleann pipe masters Liam Ó Floinn and Pat Mitchell, who travelled regularly to Miltown to listen and to learn. Pat Mitchell (author of *The Dance Music of Willie Clancy*, published by Mercier Press, 1976), cites Willie's rendering of *The Old Bucks* and *The Ravelled Hank of Yarn* on a 78 RPM Gael-Linn recording issued in 1957 as "one of the most captivating pieces of music played on the pipes that I have ever heard." Pat Mitchell was not the only musician to be utterly besotted by Willie's playing. Throughout the

Sixties and following Willie's death in 1973, many other musicians—flute players, concertina players and fiddlers—were heavily influenced by his style of piping.

Willie Clancy's classic 1950s Gael-Linn recordings helped gain him wider recognition among pipers and would-be pipers, who beat a path to west Clare to meet or play with him. Tales of legendary music sessions with Willie in Friel's kitchen and pub were legion, and hundreds of traditional music aficionados (myself included) travelled great distances to be enthralled and captivated by his piping, his songs, his stories—indeed his whole personality. For Pat Mitchell, Willie's playing of tunes epitomised the "essence of Clare music as it was described by Petrie who heard it for the first time in 1821. His tunes, even the up-tempo pieces, carried a quality of melancholia that could haunt the listener long after the music had ended. His slow airs also had that quality; played with a poignant, haunting sense of otherworld space which spoke to the human heart in a way no books or words ever could." For many, his piping ultimately was, as the nineteenth-century Clare piper Garrett Barry once described his own piping, music not for the feet but for the soul! Willie often emphasised the need to have a firm grasp of the Irish language if one was to play traditional music—particularly slow airs. These Willie would play with a deep knowledge of the airs' Irish words, his chanter articulating and accenting each nuance and shading with sensitivity, delicate grace and soul. "I feel," he told Muiris Ó Rócháin and Harry Hughes before his death, "that a knowledge of the language is essential if you are to express the true spirit of our music and, as the saying goes, Don't settle for the skim milk when the cream is at hand...." Willie never settled for the skim, producing through his piping, stories and song only the very richest of musical cream.

His sudden death in January 1973 at the age of fifty-five

was widely mourned among friends and musicians alike. So much so that it was decided by a group of his friends, among them Muiris Ó Rócháin, Harry Hughes and Tom Munnelly and aided by Breandán Breathnach and Na Píobairí Uilleann, to set up an annual summer music school in Willie's home town of Miltown Malbay as a fitting tribute and memorial to this extraordinary man and musician. (Later, the organising committee was joined by fiddler and accordionist Eamon McGivney). Their vision has become a reality. Each year, in the first week of July, acknowledged masters of the fiddle, concertina, flute, whistle, singing, dancing and, naturally, the uilleann pipes—among them fiddlers Junior Crehan, Joe Ryan, Peadar O'Loughlin and Paddy Glackin, concertina player Noel Hill, tin whistle player Mary Bergin and pipers Paddy Keenan, Ronan Browne, Pádraic Mac Mathúna, Gabriel McKeon, Seán Óg Potts and Micheál Ó Briain—descend on Miltown to demonstrate their crafts and discuss them with students. There are also pipe-making and reed-making classes run by some of the finest pipe makers at work today, including local uilleann pipe maker Nick Adams, whose fine set of B flat pipes can be heard on Pádraic Mac Mathúna's Gael-Linn album, *Hives of Honeyed Sound*. When the daily classes are over, both masters and students are free to indulge themselves in any one of the many seemingly continuous sessions in every pub in the town. Even the nearby villages of Spanish Point, Mullagh, Coor and the Crosses of Annagh get in the act, enjoying the spill-over from Miltown and generating many memorable sessions of their own.

Towards the end of June each year, as the week of the Willie Clancy Summer School approaches, there is an air of expectancy in Miltown Malbay, as its inhabitants steel themselves for another seven days and nights of music, dancing, song, talk, tears and laughter (and business of course). In cities as far flung as San Francisco and Sydney, traditional musicians too are preparing themselves for the demands—both musically and socially—which will be made of them. It will be a time for renewing old friendships, forming new ones and investigating the new or younger musicians. Most of all, it will be a time to celebrate the musical legacy bequeathed by the great musicians who are no longer with us. Willie Clancy was such a man, and as every piper blows up his bellows or every fiddler rosins his bow, his benign spirit shines through the myriad of reels, jigs, hornpipes, flings, polkas and slow airs and songs which will perfume the sweet Miltown air for those seven glorious days and nights of music.

If you should happen to be rambling through west Clare in the first week of July and you hear the sound of uilleann pipes floating on the salty air, you are close to the town of Miltown Malbay, celebrating yet again the memory of a gentle man whose music and genius has touched thousands down the years and whose soul can yet be sensed in the music of a lone piper playing one of the old dance tunes or a slow air—just as Willie might have played it.

DISCOGRAPHY:

The Music of Willie Clancy Vol 1 (Claddagh CC 32).
The Music of Willie Clancy Vol 2 (Claddagh CC 39).
The Minstrel from Clare (Topic 12T175).
The Breeze from Erin/Various(Topic 12T184).
Pipering/Various (Claddagh CC 39)
Na Ceirníní 78, 1957 — 1960/Various (Gael-Linn CEF 075).

Chapter Six

Seán Tyrrell—Twentieth-Century Bard

"For we are the stars. For we sing.
For we sing with our light.
For we are birds made of fire.
For we spread our wings over the sky.
Our light is a voice."
        Passamaquody Indian

During the summer of 1989, I worked as producer with
Davy Spillane on his *Shadow Hunter* album, and, having
agreed on the idea of featuring a guest singer on the
album, we sat down to discuss who that singer might be.
Many singers were short-listed, but after long discussions
about what choice to make, we unanimously agreed that it
just had to be a man whose praises as an instrumentalist
and more especially as a singer we had both been singing
for several years. That man was Seán Tyrrell, who is, quite
simply, the most intensely moving, soulful and talented
singer of ballads and traditional songs in Ireland today. (If
you doubt that, take a listen to his contribution to the
album mentioned above or endeavour to witness one of
his live performances.)

At the actual recording sessions, during which Seán
recorded *The Walker of the Snows*, a poem by the
nineteenth-century poet CD Shanley, and WB Yeats's *Host*

of the Air—both of which Seán has set to music—I sat again, utterly enthralled by the man's supreme command of his art and music. I had, of course, seen and heard Seán Tyrrell in noisy pub sessions in County Clare and had thrilled, along with all who listened, to his songs, delivered with great passion laced with a soulful melancholy. Now, in the clinical atmosphere of a Dublin recording studio, Seán wove again his magic spell as he faced the mike to sing Yeats's *Host of the Air*. Seán's delivery, his total command and control, his utter understanding of the piece being sung, imbued the dream-poem with an otherworld aura and quality of magic which transcended that already inherent in the piece. It was a moment I will never forget. The finished product would have, I've no doubt, pleased the poet very much. His performance of the ghostly *Walker of the Snows*, his other contribution to the album, had the same effect. I had no doubt, as I sat in that studio, my spine tingling with the power of his spell-binding performances, that here was an artist of rare quality indeed. I have heard Seán Tyrrell sing on several occasions since those studio sessions, yet each time I am wholly and utterly captivated by that strange current of electricity which passes from his heart and soul directly to his audience. It is a gift which few musicians or singers possess. Seán Tyrrell possesses this gift in abundance.

Seán Tyrell was born in 1943 into a musical family in Galway city and learned music at his father's knee. The Sixties saw him, along with Jack Geary, Henry Higgins and the now-famous songwriter Johnny Mulhern, performing regularly in the city's premier folk club—the Folk Castle. Here Seán and his fellow musicians honed their instrumental and vocal skills, rubbing shoulders with such legendary club visitors as Rambling Jack Elliot, Davy Graham and a shy young singer-songwriter who was to go on to greater things—Paul Simon. Eventually, in 1968, after a year's teaching in Belfast, Seán's itchy feet brought him to New York, where he became immersed in the Greenwich Village scene, playing in clubs such as the Bells of Hell, the Lion's Den and the Bottom Line, not to mention the interminable sessions in the Irish bars with such musicians as accordion master Joe Burke and fiddle virtuosi Paddy Cronin and Andy McGann.

Soon, the West Coast beckoned and Seán found himself in San Francisco in the early Seventies, playing banjo and mandocello alongside such Irish music greats as Joe Cooley, Kevin Keegan, and Melissa Lundy, to name but a few. In the midst of the sessions there were songs and few singers, if any, had the courage to follow Seán Tyrrell— who could silence a noisy room with his dark, rich, resonant voice. (It is a power which Seán carries still.) Those who heard him then would never forget this young Galway man, and so Seán Tyrrell's reputation as a singer of talent began to grow. 1975 saw Seán back on the East Coast—in New Hampshire, where once again he became immersed in the music scene there. During this period he became a founder-member of the group Apples in Winter, along with Jack Geary (guitar), multi-instrumentalist Tommy Mulvihill, John Tabb (bass) and Bob Emmett Fitzgerald (guitar/vocals). Together they recorded one album for Onyx, a small East Coast independent label. The album, as Seán recalls, was "not very well produced or recorded. I don't really know if it sold anywhere."

In 1975, Seán returned to Ireland, where he continued his writing and composing, although he rarely played publicly. 1978 found him working for Galway University and living in the Burren in County Clare, where he began to play on a regular basis with the legendary fiddler Tommy Peoples, Breton flautist and uilleann piper Michel Bonamy and Clare flautist Michael Hynes and guitarist Shane Holden. From time to time, uilleann piper Davy

Spillane would join their sessions in Kilfenora. Once again, Seán's power and authority as a singer stamped itself on each and every session. Once again, his rendering of songs such as the anti-war song, *The Twelfth of July*, Johnny Mulhern's *Mattie*, or the old chestnuts *The Isle of Inisfree* and *The Red River Valley*, could bring a noisy, often inattentive pub or club to a standstill. In Seán's hands, even the old, well-worn songs, such as *Red River Valley* and *Inisfree*, begin to live and breathe again with new life and soul. His unique sense of rhythm, coupled with his ability to inject a song—any song—with a special kind of magic which only he can weave, signifies clearly his place as a singer with few peers.

But what kind of singer is Seán Tyrrell? Is he a traditional singer in the pure sense of the word? A ballad singer? A contemporary singer? "I'm all of those, I suppose," is Seán's reply, "but first and foremost, I'm a singer of songs. While all my influences come directly from Irish traditional music and song, I don't sing songs from the usual ballad or traditional repertoire. I look to the great Irish poets for inspiration—such as Louis MacNeice, Jean Frazier, John Boyle O'Reilly and Charles Lever—and put their words to music; and, of course, I write songs and music myself. The words are the essence, as far as I'm concerned. But what category of singer is Seán Tyrrell? Am I a ballad singer or traditional singer? Well, somebody described me recently as an Irish blues singer. Blues is not just a black music form, it's universal. I sing the blues, I sing the Irish blues."

Some time in the early Eighties, Seán Tyrrell became fascinated with the idea of putting Brian Merriman's classic nineteenth-century poem, *The Midnight Court*, to music. The 1,206-line poem, written in Irish by the Clare poet Brian Merriman some time in the late 1700s—banned by the Catholic Church and the Irish censors for most of that period—had long since been regarded as one of the great works to survive from that century. It has been described as one of the most exuberant poems ever written in Irish or indeed in any other western European language. The poem, which has been translated many times since the first English version (by a Michael O'Shea) was published in Boston in 1897, is a celebration of the rights of women to wholesome sex and wholesome marriage. Written with a powerful mix of earthy, bawdy humour and a keen insight into male and female relationships, the poem offers us an authentic glimpse of eighteenth-century rural Irish life. It is a timeless work which strikes just as powerful a chord in modern times as it must have done when it first appeared in the early 1800s. Seán's long-held dream was to marry the David Marcus translation of the great poem to traditional music, using traditional instruments and male and female voices.

For as long as he can recall, Seán Tyrrell has been fascinated by Merriman's *Midnight Court* poem. "I was inspired by the musicality of the metre," he explains. "I felt that by putting Merriman's words to traditional music it would add another dimension to the poem. It was a dream of mine for a long while. Finally I decided to get down and do it." That inherent musicality sensed by Seán in the poem may well have stemmed from the fact that Brian Merriman was both poet and musician. In his excellent essay on Merriman, Muiris Ó Rócháin writes of him, "One manuscript says, 'He was a wild and pleasure seeking youth but an accomplished performer on the violin.'"

Seán Tyrrell's dream came true when the Druid Theatre staged *The Midnight Court* —his traditional music opera— featuring Seán alongside some fine Galway singers such as Rosie Stewart, the great traditional singer from County Fermanagh and the equally talented traditional singer and flute player Seán Keane, brother of the more famous

Dolores Keane, country-singer Bernie Mahony and Mary McPartlan from County Leitrim—as part of the 1992 Galway Arts Festival. The response, from critics and public alike, was nothing short of ecstatic. As one observer commented, having seen *The Midnight Court*, "Brian Merriman would be a delighted man if he could be here tonight to witness what has been done to his poem." Following a sell-out three-week run at the Druid, a highly successful tour of Belfast, Limerick and Cork and two historic performances in late August 1993 on the shores of Lough Graney (the original setting of the poem), *The Midnight Court*, as envisaged by Seán Tyrrell, now seems destined to run and run.

Given that Seán Tyrrell is now generally regarded as a singer with few peers, with his regular pub and club gigs crammed with committed fans, his reputation the length and breadth of the land approaching cult status, the question has been asked why there was not one record label in or out of the country with the wit or vision to sign this man to a recording contract. It is, as one reviewer put it, an impenetrable mystery, but one which is about to be resolved as this book goes to print.

After decades of life as a working musician and singer, Seán Tyrrell released his first solo album, *Cry of a Dreamer*, in March 1994.

In all civilisations of the world, the song has served as a mirror to society, reflecting the human condition. Through song, man has expressed his innermost feelings, his joys and sorrows. Through song he has sought through song to interpret his place in the world, his fears, his hopes, his dreams and his longings to transcend the mortal state. Throughout history, the bard, songwriter and singer has played an important role in society as historian, as poet, as artist and even as entertainer. The singer's role as visionary—as seer—allows us to see the fertile ground in which such imaginative possibilities grow. These days, there can be few singers in traditional, folk or rock music who can claim to be all of the above, delivering their message with simplicity, honesty and directness in the face of the tidal wave of twentieth-century pop commercialism. In Seán Tyrrell we witness such a singer/songwriter in the best bardic tradition—as historian, poet, artist, musician and entertainer.

Prepare to hear a lot more about, and from, this extraordinary singer. After over twenty-five years working as a singer/songwriter/musician and composer, Seán Tyrrell—Irish blues-ballad singer—looks set to become an overnight success. And not, it must be said, before time.

Discography:

Cry of a Dreamer/Seán Tyrrell (Long Walk Records LM 001).
Shadow Hunter/Davy Spillane (Tara CD 3023).
The Sound of Stone/Various (BAG CD 001).

Chapter Seven

Sharon Shannon—Touched by the Light

"It's only once in a generation that somebody makes a change in the way we hear a part of the culture around us, as Sharon Shannon has, and that the joy which she shares as it consumes her when she's playing is such as to transcend the sometimes pain of living in, or coming from this small patch of earth."

Eamonn McCann, *Hot Press*

"Sharon Shannon is gifted beyond rational considerations, drawing from her accordion emotions and feelings that Jimi Hendrix found in his guitar."

BP Fallon—*Sunday Tribune*

Sharon Shannon plays traditional music on a two-row Italian-made Castignari button accordion. In a country that boasts of literally hundreds of good accordion players in every county, that fact alone is no cause for celebration. There are, however, only a handful of great accordion players, and Sharon Shannon, still in her early twenties and the latest star of traditional music, must now be counted as one of the greats. Her explosion onto the national and international scene last year came as no surprise to those who have charted her extraordinary non-professional and professional playing career over the past half-dozen years or so. Coming into contact with Sharon and her music for the first time, even for those with half an ear for music, it was obvious that here was somebody very special indeed

I first heard Sharon Shannon play in a session in 1988, in a crowded McGann's Pub in Doolin in County Clare. It was immediately obvious that I was listening to a player of outstanding natural talent. Her music flowed with effortless drive, feel and grace, playing as if totally at one with her instrument and her music. Apparent too was the fact that here was a musician who possessed not only a God-given musical talent but also a much rarer quality indeed. Sharon possessed and exuded that will-o'-the-wisp quality that even transcends natural talent—innate charisma. From within the circle of players, all wholly and absolutely involved in the tunes, Sharon's own shining personality pierced through the wall of sound as a beacon of bright light through an Atlantic sea-fog. While the other players adopted a serious mien while playing their instruments, Sharon's sense of sheer delight and joy as she played was infectious. Her magnetic physical presence in the session, though never domineering, seemed to make a vital difference, both to her fellow musicians and her listeners, as her music sent shivers of electricity down collective spines. In that moment, as she wove her magic spell on all present, she seemed to me almost to possess an otherworld aura; delicate, subtle, undefinable, but definitely present. Also in that moment, I truly felt that here was one of those rare persons gifted beyond normal, a person truly touched by the light. Today, six years later, as Sharon enjoys the accolades now being showered on her, those qualities are still very much in evidence in her stage and record performances.

Sharon Shannon was born twenty-four years ago near the village of Corrofin in north Clare. Growing up in a family steeped in traditional music in an area famous for its rich musical heritage and culture, it was only natural that Sharon should take up an instrument. The instrument she chose was the two-row button accordion. Her sister Majella chose the fiddle, Mary the banjo, and older brother Gary the concert flute, and all are now highly skilled practitioners. Apart from home influences, Sharon's chief early influence and tutor was the highly-respected local fiddle-player and music teacher, Frank Custy. He recalls hearing Sharon for the first time: "I was interested in horses and used to borrow a horse-box from IJ Shannon, Sharon's father. Every time I rang the Shannon house, this kid in the background was playing the accordion. If it was nine o'clock in the morning or nine in the evening the accordion was going in the background. That was Sharon, who was maybe ten or so at the time. She came to classes later and has since said that they freed up her playing and gave her a sense of fun while playing. The kind of ability she had, I couldn't touch or improve on. She had great natural talent, but she also worked hard—very hard—at her playing...that mustn't be forgotten. From the moment I first heard her I knew she had the golden touch." Sharon's vivacious personal and musical energy spilled over through her music, affecting all who played with her or listened to her. Frank Custy recalls, "When I sat down to play with her, you'd feel this power...this energy...coming from her. She played with the drive and confidence of a much older musician and at this stage, she was still just a kid!"

At the tender age of fourteen, she was a member of the group Disert Tola, made up of Frank Custy's star pupils, travelling to the US on short tours. While still at school, Sharon found her way to Doolin, the "Mecca" of traditional music, drawn by the lure of contact with the scores of traditional musicians who gravitated towards the tiny north Clare village. It was here, in the company of musicians such as master fiddler Tommy Peoples, uilleann piper

Davy Spillane, and bouzouki player Owen O'Neill, that Sharon honed her style and developed her repertoire of tunes from countless hours' session playing. During this period she admits to not having had a clue what to do with her life, apart from the endless music sessions in Doolin and in nearby villages. Her music captivated the ear of award-winning film director Jim Sheridan (*My Left Foot*, *The Field*), who invited her to provide music for, and tour with, his production of the Brendan Behan classic work *The Hostage* for the Druid Theatre, Galway. When the touring ended, Sharon was back in Doolin or Galway, popping up with her accordion wherever there was the slightest whiff of a music session.

Fate was to play a hand, however, in the shape of Steve Wickham, fiddle player with The Waterboys, who met and heard Sharon on a visit to Doolin. Soon after Wickham's return to Dublin, singing Sharon's praises to all who would hear, she joined the newly-formed Arcady, which also featured ex-De Danann bodhrán-man Johnny McDonagh and singer Frances Black. A year later, however, Sharon accepted an invitation from Waterboy front-man Mike Scott to join the group, catapulting her from the world of pure traditional music to Scott's world of contemporary acoustic folk-rock. It was also a world of international concert tours, with all the attendant media pressures and hype. It was a far cry indeed from the free-and-easy life of a session player in Doolin, but it served to introduce Sharon to the life of a professional musician on the road while expanding her musical appreciation outside and beyond pure traditional music. Of her time with The Waterboys Sharon says, "It was musically brilliant for me, a fantastic experience."

In 1990, with the experience of being a Waterboy behind her, Sharon embarked on her first solo album, under the watchful and experienced eye of manager/

producer John Dunford. The album, *Sharon Shannon* (Solid Records), released in 1992 and featuring some of the biggest stars of Irish rock and traditional music (Donal Lunny, Tommy Hayes, Mike Scott, Adam Clayton, Liam Ó Maonlaí and Trevor Hutchinson), burst on the contemporary music scene like a breath of fresh air. On this, her debut solo album, Sharon's nimble fingers dance around Portuguese tunes, Cajun, French-Canadian pieces and Irish reels, all meshing together to a backdrop of contemporary sounds and rhythms, which was described as "a wondrous thing" by one music reviewer. Within a few weeks the album had gone into the Top Ten Album charts and was drawing rave reviews from papers both at home and abroad. To date, the album is reported to have sold over 40,000 copies, a massive achievement for any Irish act, rock, traditional, or otherwise. Following her chart success came the awards-voted top Irish Folk and Traditional Artist in the *Hot Press* readers' poll (ahead of Christy Moore, Mary Black and Enya), and she was voted third in the Irish Musician poll (behind the Edge and Van the Man). The Edge was to list Sharon's album among his top ten all-time favourite albums in *Rolling Stone*. The album went platinum in Ireland after six months. This represents unprecedented sales figures for a totally instrumental album.

Since then, Sharon's life has shifted to permanent high gear; touring constantly to meet the demands of a fast-growing international audience of fans. Her inclusion, along with Eleanor McEvoy, Dolores Keane, Maura O'Connell and Mary and Frances Black, in the phenomenally successful album, *A Woman's Heart* (Dara Records), released in the summer of 1992, no doubt helped it on its way to being the biggest-selling Irish album ever and winning her new fans along the way. In the meantime, her touring schedule went into top gear: Galway one night,

London the next, followed by New York or Boston. At the first Celtic Music Festival held in San Francisco in early March 1992, an audience of over 4,000 got a taste of the Shannon magic when Sharon and her band (which includes ex-Waterboy Trevor Hutchinson on double-bass, Paul Kelly on fiddle and Gerry O'Beirne on guitar) took the place by storm. Some months later, at the Seville Expo 92, Sharon's exuberant music moved Spanish feet and hearts, winning new fans at every performance. It's a similar story everywhere she plays. As 1992 came to a close, *The Late Late Show,* hosted by Gay Byrne, dedicated an entire programme to Sharon and her music. If there were any viewers who doubted Sharon's talent or ability to weave a magic of a very special kind prior to the show, there were certainly none afterwards.

1993 has seen Sharon Shannon further consolidate her position as one of the most charismatic, appealing and successful figures on the Irish music scene. Her profile continues to grow both at home and abroad. This is backed up by heavy touring schedules and headlining appearances at all the major musisc festivals, such as sharing top billing with Bob Dylan, Joan Baez, Van Morrison, Jerry Lee Lewis, The Chieftains, Luka Bloom and Shane McGowan at the massive three-day Fleadh Mór music-extravaganza at Tramore in County Waterford.

Sharon Shannon plays Irish traditional music on the button accordion. She also plays Scottish, French, Canadian, Cajun and Bulgarian music with confidence and commanding ease. Coming through her dazzling virtuosity at all times is her infectious bubbling personality. But behind her appealing aura of pixie-like vulnerability and gentleness lies a strength of character, quiet confidence and self-awareness. These are qualities she may have to dip into to weather the often rough seas of life as a professional musician. But whatever the weather, Sharon

Shannon's strength of personality, coupled with her extraordinary ability to weave a magical web of music, will overcome any future highs and lows she may face as a much sought-after rising star of international status.

Sharon Shannon is, quite simply, a musician of exceptional talent and personal charisma. It is a talent and charisma that will, as one writer admitted, "leave you both stunned and amazed," as indeed I was when I first heard her in a Doolin pub in 1988 and when I last heard her, bewitching and enthralling thousands from a San Francisco Festival stage early last year. Through her music and vivacious personality, she continues to radiate a vitality and charm that has truly touched our collective heart-strings in a way few other individuals, or indeed events, could.

"It remains true," wrote John Waters in a perceptive *Irish Times* essay (29 June 1993), celebrating the successes of contemporary Irish music, "that in Ireland today, if you want to know how people feel, you are better off listening to Sharon Shannon's *Coridinio*...than sitting through *Saturday View.*"

Please don't miss seeing or hearing Sharon Shannon, wizard of the two-row button-accordion. It will be an experience that will stay with you for a long, long time to come.

Discography:

Sharon Shannon/Sharon Shannon (Solid Records ROCD 8).
A Woman's Heart/Various (Dara DARTE CD 158).
Bringing It All Back Home/Various (Hummingbird HB CD 001).

Chapter Eight

The Kilfenora Céilí Band—87 Years of Music-Making

Sundays in the north Clare village of Kilfenora, situated on the edge of the Burren, are normally quiet and peaceful, the tranquillity broken only by the hum of light local traffic or tourist traffic en route to the Cliffs of Moher or the nearby Spa town of Lisdoonvarna. Sunday 4 July 1992 was an exception, a day that will be recalled by inhabitants and visitors alike as a day to remember. For on this glorious summer Sunday, an air of Mediterranean festivity permeated the town of Kilfenora, whose inhabitants turned out to pay tribute to their most famous sons and daughters. It was a day when musicians, supporters and well-wishers gathered to celebrate the town's most famous export, the Kilfenora Céilí Band. There was good cause to celebrate: the Kilfenora Céilí Band had just chalked up its eighty-fifth year in existence.

For several generations the county of Clare, especially north Clare, has been an acknowledged stronghold of traditional music. In recent times the villages of Doolin and Miltown Malbay in west Clare have attracted thousands of visitors from the United States and Europe, who travel great distances to experience first-hand this rich, living tradition and culture (a fact, incidentally, that Bord Fáilte seem unable, or unwilling, to fully appreciate and address positively). Ironically, most of these travellers on their way to Doolin or Miltown would have by-passed the village that for several generations kept the flame of traditional music and dance alight and nurtured in north Clare. For, more than any other, it was the village of Kilfenora which was at the very core of a vibrant and passionately involved nucleus of musicians which retained and shaped a unique musical inheritance. That passion led a handful of musicians to form a small band initially to raise funds for the local church and later to play at local house and crossroad dances. The year was 1907, and today, eighty-seven years, the Kilfenora Céilí Band still around, albeit without any original member, to lift the spirit and move the feet with its own very special brand of traditional dance music. Few other dance-bands, regardless of musical genre, can lay claim to such a proud and remarkable history.

No living person around Kilfenora can remember a time when the playing of traditional music was not the most important social and cultural activity in the area. Music, and musicians, always seem to have flourished there, regardless of political or economic or social changes which have occurred from Famine times to the present day. The original band of 1907 boasted the cream of local players, mainly recruited from local musical families, the Lynchs, Wards, Mulqueeneys and McMahons. Concertina virtuoso Brigid McGrath (née Lynch) was there at the beginning, and so too was her brother John Joe Lynch and Austin Tierney, whose sons PJ and Gus, respectively, carried on the tradition and made up the nucleus of the famous Fifties band. Also included were PJ Lynch's brother Jerry on accordion, Paddy Mullins on flute and the legendary Kitty Linnane (PJ and Jerry's first cousin) on piano. Another cousin to join was Jimmy Ward, who played banjo, proving that the family that plays together stays together. The late Jimmy once commented on the band's special musical rapport: "I think what helped us was the fact that we were all neighbours and the families...such as the Wards and the Lynches...had been playing together since the beginning of the century.... We knew each other well...we could time together well...we wouldn't want to be told that we stuck dancers to the floor." Other members at this time included Frank Mahony, Jim Mulqueeny, Gus Teirney, Pat Madigan, Tom Eustace, Gerard O'Loughlin and Jim McCormack.

The Fifties was the golden era of céilí dancing, and, though they had serious competition in bands like the Liverpool Céilí Band, the Tulla Céilí Band from east Clare, the Aughrim Slopes Céilí Band and the Ballinakill Céilí Band from south Galway and the Laichtín Naofa Céilí Band from Miltown Malbay (which included fiddler Junior Crehan, Michael Falsy and JC Talty on flutes and Martin Talty on pipes), the Kilfenora Band dominated the Irish music dancing scene. Having run off with three of the All-Ireland Céilí Band titles from three consecutive All-Ireland Fleadhs (1954/55/56), the Kilfenora Céilí Band ruled supreme as Ireland's best-loved traditional dance-band, filling dance-halls the length and breath of the country. Kitty Linnane remembered the period with affection. "We would all pile in to one car, instruments and whatever sound gear we carried at the time and drive to all corners of the country, play for hours and drive back home to Kilfenora afterwards. And all for thirty shillings (£1.50) or so!" All this was achieved at a time when rampant emigration stalked the land (as it did in the post-Famine period and as it does today), and hearing genuine Irish traditional music on the radio was as rare as hens' teeth. The band's immediately identifiable and unique sound, coupled with their uncanny sense of rhythm (derived from generations of a family and extended family's music-making), gave, as one dancer described, "your feet such a jolt that you couldnt help but get up and dance to their music. There was no band anywhere to touch them for rhythm and lift." For the band, it was a door which swung both ways. Kitty Linnane was often to comment that having good dancers to play for was vital for the bands famous lift and rhythm. "Wherever and whenever we played," Kitty was to recall, "we looked out for one good group of set-dancers in front of the stage and we played to that set all evening. It was the dancers who gave us the rhythm, and as long as they kept dancing, we kept playing."

Wherever it came from, the Kilfenora Band possessed and injected a powerful and dynamic rhythmic drive into their music. It was a rhythm, lift and indeed flair that attracted thousands to the dance-halls at home and more especially in England, where the band regularly played to packed halls of Irish emigrants and London Irish. Their London appearances, at venues such as the famous Galtymore in Cricklewood and the Fulham Broadway, both in south London, were akin to modern pop concerts, such were the huge number of Irish attending and the excitement generated as the old Clare reels and jigs moved tired spirits and feet. Kitty Linnane recalls meeting whole families, forced to emigrate from around Kilfenora, at these London venues during the Sixties, while in Ireland numbers attending declined steadily. "Sometimes it was like coming home. We used to meet all our own neighbours from Clare and people we knew from other counties. I suppose we gave them a little touch of home. It was quite sad really."

Three albums were recorded in the Sixties and early Seventies, which go some way to capturing the true energy, verve and atmosphere of their live performances; though one would have to be physically present to experience fully the electricity and magic that was the Kilfenora Band at the peak of its power and fame. The recordings made then by the band were done in one afternoon recording session. A recording of a complete album in three or four hours was common. The band gathered in the studio (for one album it was a hotel room in Ennis), sat as they would on stage, an overall sound balance was obtained by the recording engineer, and the session would get under way, the band playing through their prepared repertoire of reels, jigs, hornpipes and songs with no re-takes. (Similar modern recording sessions can take many days.) Because of these primitive recording techniques, many of the recordings were poorly balanced and mixed. Notwithstanding these constraints, the essential spark, rhythm and verve of the band shine through even the most technically woolly of their recorded work. One of those albums, recorded in the late Sixties, features ex-Bothy Band fiddle-master, Tommy Peoples, who had joined the band having married Kitty Linnane's daughter Marie in the early Sixties. Their vocalist at that time was the young Miltown Malbay singer-guitarist PJ Murrihy, who is now a famous recording artist in his own right.

The sweeping social changes brought about in the Sixties made life difficult for working céilí bands, the Kilfenora included. For a time it seemed that the céilí band was in danger of becoming extinct in the heady climate of the post-Beatle Pop-culture. Dancers deserted Irish dancing as céilí bands gave way to the showband, the rock and beat-group and later to the ubiquitous disco. Added to that was the emergence of The Chieftains in the Sixties and later Planxty, De Danann and The Bothy Band in the Seventies, whose tightly arranged music appealed primarily to a listening audience. It was not a good time for céilí bands and céilí dancing in Ireland. But as other céilí bands threw in the towel, the Kilfenora tightened its belt and soldiered on, regardless of current trends or directions. Their public appearances were confined to regular local pub venues or céilís organised at Christmas-time to cater for the returned emigrants. Clearly, the glue that bonded the band in the Seventies and Eighties and was to see it through thick and thin was the same as it was in the depression decades of the Thirties, Forties and Fifties. That glue consisted of a burning love and passion for the music, and the musicians' desire to play music for its own sake. Another important element in that glue is the great driving force behind the band for over thirty years or so—piano player Kitty Linnane. Through the highs and lows, Kitty's organising skill and sheer dedication to the task of keeping the Kilfenora sound alive, have contributed greatly to the band's survival.

Kitty Linnane's contribution, and indeed that of the many band members who played with the Kilfenora band down the years, was recognised fully at the eighty-fifth anniversary celebrations, which was broadcast live on RTE One radio on 4 July 1992. Apart from Kitty and the other surviving Fifties members (fiddlers PJ Lynch and Gus Tierney and flute player Paddy Mullins, born around the time the original band formed in 1907), the stage was filled with any player who had, at any time, played with the band over the last three decades. To hear that special sound, which only the Kilfenora musicians could produce, fill the square of the village that gave the band its name was both thrilling and moving and will be remembered by those who witnessed it for many years to come.

At the edge of the Kilfenora square, on that glorious Sunday morning, a couple in their late fifties danced a figure of a set as Kitty Linnane led in with her distinctive two piano chords and the band played again some of the old tunes with the old, powerful and energetic lift and rhythm that made the band famous in the Fifties. It's a fair guess to say the couple probably had met, courted and danced their young lives away to the Kilfenora Céilí Band. At another corner of the square a group of young children twirled, skipped and spun at the sheer excitement and delight of it all. One misty-eyed old man, watching and listening to the assembled gathering of musicians from a distance, removed his pipe, shook his head and remarked, "Will you listen to that music. They sound as mighty as they did forty years ago. We won't see their likes again!" It was a sentiment that the thousands of fans of the Kilfenora Céilí Band the world over would no doubt share.

Kitty Linnane passed away on 15 March 1993. She was laid to rest in the ancient cathedral churchyard of her native Kilfenora on St Patrick's Day to the sound of fiddles playing the old Kilfenora tunes she loved so well. It was exactly as she would have wanted it to be. May she rest in peace.

Discography:

Clare Céilí/The Kilfenora Céilí Band (EMI Stal 1013).
The Kilfenora Céilí Band (Pickwick HPC 606).
The Kilfenora Céilí Band (Transatlantic TRA 283).
The Kilfenora Céilí Band (Shamrock SLP 904).

Chapter Nine

Clare Women Concertina Players

In a small, dimly-lit pub in a west Clare village, a group of attentive listeners gather around an elderly lady seated quietly in a corner. The year is 1958 and some of the people gathered here have travelled from as far away as Dublin to sit in the presence of this famous woman. They now concentrate fully on this smiling lady, seated and unmoving except for her nimble fingers, which dance effortlessly across the keys of a tiny concertina cradled in her lap. Her name is Mrs Crotty, born Elizabeth Markham near Cooraclare in west Clare in 1885, a virtuoso player by any standards but exceptional in the Fifties and early Sixties in that she was one one of the small number of players who is a well-known name, a celebrity in traditional music circles. Even more exceptional at that time was the fact that she was a woman player, one of only a very small number of women publicly playing Irish traditional music.

Young Elizabeth Markham grew up in a home in southwest Clare that was filled with music. Her mother played the fiddle and her older sister, Maggie, played the Anglo-concertina, the most common in use at that time, and Lizzie had soon mastered the rudiments of the instrument. Soon after that she was playing for local house dances, alongside her mother and sister.

In 1914 she married Jack Crotty and moved to Kilrush, where they ran a pub which was to become a Mecca for musicians in the Forties and Fifties in the thriving market town. Mrs Crotty had to wait for the Fifties before her reputation as a gifted concertina player spread to all parts of the country. Her appearances at various fleadhs and her subsequent broadcasts on Ciarán Mac Mathúna's radio programmes earned her a countrywide reputation as a concertina-player to be reckoned with. Elizabeth Crotty died at the height of her fame in 1960.

In the decades which preceded the relatively liberal Sixties, the patriarchal essence of the society in which Mrs Crotty and her fellow women musicians moved offered stark choices. The rules were simple, and rigid. A woman's place was in the home. Rarely were women seen in bars and pubs in rural Ireland and rarer still was the sight of a woman traditional player in a music session. That is not to suggest that there were no women players. There were in fact a great number of superb women musicians and singers up and down the country, but their talents were restricted to the privacy of their own homes These women took down their instruments only to entertain at house-dances, parties at Christmas and Easter-time or for weddings, christenings and wake, particularly for the infamous American wakes. In any house which possessed an instrument, and there were many in Kerry, Clare and Galway, where the most popular instruments were the fiddle and the concertina, you were sure to find a woman player. Mrs Crotty was one such player. So too were the legendary fiddlers Aggie White from east Galway and Julia Clifford from Kerry.

An equally gifted Clare concertina player was Mrs Brigid McGrath from near Kilfenora. Unlike Mrs Crotty, Brigid McGrath was rarely heard outside her own home. She was never recorded, but her tunes have found their way into the general traditional repertoire, and she remains a legendary, if shadowy, figure among Clare musicians, especially concertina-players. Mrs McGrath was born Brigid Lynch in 1880 in Clogher, near Kilfenora. She was the sister of John Joe Lynch, one of the founders of the Kilfenora Céilí Band, which included Brigid on concertina and Austin Tierney on fiddle.

As Mrs Crotty's reputation in South Clare grew among listeners and musicians, so too did Brigid McGrath's in north Clare. The late Gerry McMahon, Brigid's cousin and also a respected musician, recalled her being able to "get magic notes from an old concertina held together with tape and bits of cord. She could get music from a board." She also wrote tunes. According to Gerry McMahon, "She slept with a pencil tied to the leg of her bed. She would wake from a dream with a tune in her head and so as to remember it in the morning, she would scribble the notes of the tune on the wallpaper beside her bed. Then, when she got up in the morning, she would pick up the concertina and play the notes written on the wall. Many a good tune came that way." Perhaps it was in this way that one of her best-known tunes came into existence. The tune, now known as *Mulqueeney's Hornpipe*, can be heard on the Mulligan album by Matt Molloy, Tommy Peoples and Paul Brady (1978), and on a Chieftains album recorded in the Eighties. It was composed by Mrs McGrath some time in the Thirties and later popularised by her fiddle-playing cousin Jim Mulqueeney, who in turn passed it on to other north Clare musicians. As was common among many traditional musicians of that era who were composing tunes, Mrs McGrath would have been reluctant to admit publicly to writing new tunes, and therefore her pieces would have been quickly absorbed into the traditional repertoire and played by other musicians as such. She died in 1948 but her reputation as a great concertina player lives on, and her influence on both north Clare music and musicians has been enormous.

In 1984, in a small commercial recording studio in Dublin, a group of assorted musicians gathered together to make a historic recording. Historic, because the group, who called themselves Macalla, comprised no less than twenty-three women, the cream of young Irish traditional musicians and singers. Among those present were fiddlers Edel McWeeney, Roma Casey and Mairéad Ní Mhaonaigh (of Altan fame), flute players Catherine McGorman and Clodagh McRory and Mary McNamara, a young concertina-player from County Clare.

Mary is one of the finest young concertina players to emerge in the last two decades. Her playing is gentle and graceful yet wonderfully eloquent and rich in the tradition of her native east Clare. Born into a musical household in the town of Tulla, the heartland of traditional music in east Clare, Mary was steeped in music from the day she was born. Her father played concertina and her mother, though she didn't play an instrument, carried in her head a large repertoire of tunes which she later passed on to Mary, her late brother PJ and Andrew, who is currently one of the best-known accordion players in Clare. Mary's introduction to the concertina came at about the age of ten. "My father had bought a German concertina for my grand-aunt Minnie Murphy in the hope that she would start playing again after years of not playing because of bad arthritis. At this stage I, along with my two brothers, was playing the accordion. Minnie decided the concertina was too stiff and she asked if we would take it home for her and loosen it out for her. We did and I was the one that took to it. I fell in love with it and Minnie never got it back."

One of her first teachers and strongest influences was a local concertina player, Mickey Donoghue. "Mickey played in a very gentle manner and I feel that I owe my present style to the many sessions as a young player with him." The first tune she remembers learning was the reel, *The Ships Are Sailing*. Another influence on her style and repertoire was the legendary uilleann piper Martin Rochford from Broadford. "Martin had strange versions of tunes which I'm proud to say I still play today." Mary was fortunate too in that she was but a stone's-throw away from some of the other great east Clare traditional musicians, fiddlers P Joe Hayes and Paddy Canny, tin whistle player Joe Bane and Bill Maley. In this fertile ground of traditional music, Mary honed her concertina playing craft to a fineness unmatched by other practitioners.

Her musical world was to change dramatically in 1978 when she and her Wheatstone concertina moved to Dublin. Her first experience of playing at a session was one she will not forget. "My first session was in the Comhaltas HQ in Monkstown," Mary recalls, "and there were about twenty musicians playing away like the hammers of Hell! Having found the courage to take out the concertina and join in, I found I didn't know any of the modern session tunes they were playing—all my tunes were east Clare tunes. I had to put my concertina back in its box. I went out the very next day, bought O'Neill's 1001 and learned the bones of it off by heart." With most of O'Neill's tunes in her current repertoire, Mary is still happiest when playing the tunes she grew up with in her native east Clare.

There is now much discussion on how traditional music has changed over the years. Mary agrees that concertina playing certainly has changed over the years since Mrs Crotty's day, with the emphasis now on technique rather than style. "Many of the younger players want to be able to play brilliantly rather than nicely," she comments, "and this may be the reason why so many concertina players sound the same today."

Today Mary McNamara is considered, along with Miriam Collins and Dympna O'Sullivan, two other superb Clare concertina players, to be among the finest virtuoso concertina players in Ireland. Though she rarely plays at informal sessions, when she does it is in the company of like-minded musicians that she feels most comfortable with. She can also be found passing on her lore to concertina students at each Willie Clancy Summer School in Miltown Malbay. Apart from her inclusion on the 1984 Macalla album, Mary has remained unrecorded, apart from regular radio and television appearances. That situation is about to change with a forthcoming album on the Claddagh label which also features one of her old musical heroes and mentors P Joe Hayes and his son Martin, on fiddles. Her strong Clare background in music and her outgoing, happy personality is indelibly stamped on her buoyant, spirited style. As with Mrs Crotty and Mrs McGrath before her, Mary McNamara responds to a deep inner pulse and musical voice that speaks to us from a different age, an age when the specific value of each note, each delicate nuance, each subtle variation was savoured and appreciated by both player and listener for its own sake. She has inherited all the richness, vitality and spirit of a great Clare concertina tradition and will confidently carry that tradition into the next century.

It has been a long road for traditional music and the women who play it. Elizabeth Crotty and Brigid McGrath would be pleased, and perhaps a little astonished, at the popularity presently enjoyed by such an unassuming instrument as the concertina. One thing is certain: as long as concertina players such as Miriam Collins, Dympna

O'Sullivan and Mary McNamara continue to play, the spirit and soul that permeated the bitter-sweet music of Mrs Crotty and Mrs McGrath and the many unnamed Clare women players of the past will continue to raise the heart.

Discography:

Mary McNamara/Mary McNamara (Claddagh CL 60 CD).

Chapter Ten

Noel Hill—King of the Irish Concertina

For most people, the suggestion of a concertina conjures up the Hollywood-created images of Jolly-Jack-Tar sailors, fortified with their rum-tots, tripping it out aboard ship to the sound of a badly-played concertina offering of the Sailor's Hornpipe. In short, it is an instrument that, for many, is not to be taken seriously. Unless, that is, you happen to be a fan of Irish traditional music or have had the unforgettable experience of witnessing Ireland's greatest living concertina player—Clare-born Noel Hill. Still in his early thirties, Noel Hill has been a legend in traditional music circles since he emerged on the scene almost twenty years ago. Whenever and wherever traditional players, and in particular traditional concertina players, are discussed, Noel Hill's name is mentioned time and time again. His work, both as a solo recording artist and with the cream of traditional and contemporary musicians such as Tony Linnane, Tony MacMahon, Matt Molloy, Planxty, Christy Moore, Mick Hanly and Mairéad Ní Dhomhnaill, has earned him the well-deserved title of master of the Irish concertina.

Coming as he does from a county which has produced some of the most celebrated traditional concertina players ever—John Kelly, Solas Lillis, Tom Carey, Tommy McCarthy, Mrs Crotty, Paddy Murphy, Bernard O'Sullivan,

Sonny Murrey, Chris Droney, Packie Russell—it is a title which is not earned, or indeed bestowed, lightly.

It is indeed true that there are more concertinas and concertina players per square mile in County Clare than in any other county in Ireland. Why this should be is a question which has not yet been answered.

The concertina was invented in or around 1820 and evolved over the next twenty years to become the instrument in general use today. Sir Charles Wheatstone, the English physicist, patented his version of the concertina in 1844, making it, according to broadcaster Ciarán Mac Mathúna, the only instrument invented by an Englishman. There are two types of concertina, the English, in which the note is the same whether you press or draw on any particular key, and the Anglo-German, in which the note will be different, similar to a chromatic accordion. The concertina is said to have found its way to Clare with the return of soldiers from the Napoleonic Wars or from sailors coming ashore from the ships berthing along the Shannon estuary around the turn of the century. Some say it arrived in the mid-1800s; others claim the late 1800s. Whichever is true, the fact remains that the concertina has become so popular in Clare that, for several decades now, the county is synonymous with the instrument.

From 1900 on the concertina gained ground rapidly. Compared to the pipes or fiddle, the concertina was cheap, it did not require much upkeep, it was portable and was an ideal instrument for players, especially women, who were not professional musicians. Walk into practically any household in north, west or east Clare from 1920 onwards and you would be sure to see a fiddle hung over the fireplace, but walk into any house in south or south-west Clare and you were sure to find a concertina. (This writer witnessed six concertina players at a house session in Kilmaley in 1976.) The concertina was taken down at the end of a long day's work to move the young and old to dance, to ease and lift troubled spirits, to while away summer evenings or long winter nights or to express the longings and loneliness of the human heart. Throughout the Thirties, Forties and Fifties, their sweet reedy notes were as common to the cottages of south and west County Clare as the smell of fresh thatch or the perfumed aroma of the smoke from open turf fires.

Noel Hill's home in Caherea, eight miles south-west of Ennis, was one such house. Both his parents and grandparents, his aunts and uncles, all played the concertina. Born in the late Fifties into this rich musical atmosphere, it seemed only natural that Noel should absorb this vibrant family heritage and learn the concertina.

"It was most logical that I should take to the concertina," Noel explains; "everybody around me at home, and many of the neighbours, all played the concertina. I tried playing a fiddle that was in the house, but there was no unconscious instruction coming through to tell me that this was the instrument for me. As soon as I picked up the concertina, I could bring out tunes. It seemed to be moulded to my body. Right away I knew instinctively that the concertina was the instrument for me."

Later, Noel came under the influence of the great Paddy Murphy from Connolly, some six miles away from the Hill household. Another major influence was his uncle, Paddy Hill, who also played a Wheatstone concertina. His uncle Paddy would accompany Noel to Paddy Murphy's house on long winter nights to sit by the Murphy fireside to talk, but more important, to listen and to learn from one of the great concertina masters of the day. When Noel wasn't visiting Paddy Murphy in his home, Paddy would visit the Hills' home, especially around Christmas for the regular house-dance and party usually held between Christmas Day and New Year's Day. Noel also remembers several other well-known musicians visiting:

"Our house had the reputation of being a music house. Apart from Paddy Murphy, who was a regular visitor, I well remember fiddler Paddy Canny coming from east Clare. Peadar O'Loughlin, who lived close by, visited a lot and so did the piper Seán Reid. So I had a lot of music recorded in my head from listening to these musicians play; even long before I started on the concertina. Indeed a lot of the music I play today comes from listening to those players in our house."

From the moment Noel received his first concertina (purchased by his mother in nearby Ennis), he quickly developed his technique, building up a huge repertoire of tunes in an uncompetitive, unpressurised, homely atmosphere which allowed him to fully understand and appreciate the true nature, soul and depth of the music around him. In the fullest sense of the word, Noel absorbed not only the music, but also the essence of the tradition through which the music was transmitted.

A chance meeting with another immensely talented young musician in the late Sixties was to shape Noel's musical life for the following decade or more. While attending a music class run by the famous Toonagh music teacher, Frank Custy, he came into contact with another music student from the neighbouring village of Corrofin. For as long as anybody could recall, Tony Linnane was able to play traditional music. Before he could walk, he had taken an interest in music. At the age of three or four, he had a command of the harmonica which stunned amazed listeners. Later, Tony switched to fiddle and by his early teens his reputation as a musician of exceptional talent was known far beyond his native Corrofin in north

Clare.

On the invitation of Tony's father, Pat Linnane, a man whose passion and love of traditional music was the driving force of his life, Noel Hill visited the Linnane home in Corrofin. Immediately, a personal friendship and musical rapport was formed between the two teenagers and a strong musical bond forged. The fruits of this kinship can be heard on Noel and Tony's first recorded album from 1979. Released on the Tara label and titled simply *Noel Hill and Tony Linnane* (Tara 2006), which also featured flute-player Matt Molloy, Alec Finn and Micheál Ó Domhnaill, the album was hailed as a masterpiece. Here were two young musicians whose playing is mature, powerful and confident and whose music reflected the strong traditions and musical values which had shaped them.

"When I hear the album now," Noel reflects, "I think it's a very innocent recording. It certainly reflects the way we were and the phrasing and tempo of Clare music."

It was certainly an album which captured their sheer virtuosity and vitality. The innocence Noel refers to is perhaps an over-critical assessment of an album which is universally regarded as a classic traditional music recording and still sought after and enjoyed by fans of superb, honest traditional music. Prior to that album, the duo had spent some time in the group Inchiquin, which also featured fellow Clareman Kieran Hanrahan on banjo and Tony Callanan on guitar and vocals. The group toured Germany, recorded one album (now deleted), but broke up in 1978—Hanrahan and Callanan going on to form Stockton's Wing. Noel and Tony were then joined for a brief period by Barry Moore, a.k.a. Luka Bloom, before returning to work in the way which best suited their musical vision—as a concertina-fiddle duet.

Tours, sessions and other recordings soon followed,

and Noel and Tony's unique blend of concertina and fiddle were heard live in concerts both at home and abroad and on record with Christy Moore's *The Iron Behind the Velvet* (Tara 2002, 1978) and Planxty's *The Woman I Loved So Well* (Tara 3005,1980).

The Eighties brought increased pressures on the duo. Noel was by now committed to life as a professional musician, probably the first and only professional concertina player in the country. "I never worked at a job that didn't involve music. I didn't set out to be a professional musician, it just worked out that way."

Their split, actually more of a slow drift apart, finally came about when Noel moved to Dublin and Tony opted to stay and work outside music in his native Clare.

Since then, Noel has ploughed a solo furrow, taking his trusty Wheatstone or Jeffries concertinas across continents —from Stockholm to San Francisco, from Miltown Malbay to Milwaukee; making new fans along the way and exposing fresh ears to his marvellous music, made on this small but princely instrument. Two classic albums have been produced in that time. One album, with renowned accordion player Tony MacMahon, *I gCnoc na Graí*, 1985 (Gael-Linn CEF 114), captures the energy of a country house-dance or pub session in all its exuberant glory. If an Irish traditional album has been recorded which captures so fully the very heart and soul of the tradition, this writer had not yet heard it.

Noel's long-awaited solo album, *The Irish Concertina* (Claddagh Records CCF 21), arrived in 1988 and went on to win the Irish Folk Album of the Year Award. Quite simply it is a tour-de-force recording. Here we have a stylist who has taken his instrument to new heights without compromising the tradition from which he springs. His playing of tunes such as *The Gold Ring, The Pigeon on the*

Gate and *The Moving Cloud* is quite magnificent. Noel shapes each tune as a finely sculpted piece of intricate musical art, delicacy and beauty. These are tunes tinged too with a melancholic sadness. In his hands even the most buoyant of tunes is at times imbued with an atmosphere of gentle sorrow, regret and loss, executed with wonderful elegance and precision, grace and flow. Here is concertina playing as you have never heard it before—in any tradition.

As Noel Hill, professional concertina player, prepares to take his music to new audiences he revels in the prospect of forthcoming work as a solo traveller and performer. He says, "I honestly believe that traditional music at its best is played solo. The next best to that is duets and then trios and so on. But the music that most appeals to me is the solo player or the solo singer. That's the fuel that rises my heart."

Noel Hill and his concertina seem set to supply that musical fuel to raise the spirit of countless human hearts for many years to come. What better can be said of any musician? One thing is sure: on hearing Noel Hill as he continues to expand the boundaries of the concertina and up the ante for any future concertina players, any images of the Jolly-Jack-Tar and his jokey concertina will be dispelled for ever.

Discography:

The Irish Concertina/Noel Hill (Claddagh CCF 21).
Noel Hill and Tony Linnane/Noel Hill and Tony Linnane (Tara 2006).
The Iron Behind the Velvet/Christy Moore (Tara 2002).
The Woman I Loved So Well/Planxty (Tara 3005).
I gCnoc na Graí/Noel Hill and Tony MacMahon (Gael-

Linn CEF 114).

The Fourth Irish Folk Festival on the Road/Noel Hill (IINT 180-038).

The Green Fields of America/Noel Hill (CCE DL19).

H-Block/Various Artists/Noel Hill (HB LP 001).

Aislingí Ceoil—Music of Dreams/Noel Hill, Tony Mac *Mahon and Iarla Ó Lionaird* (Gael-Linn CEFC/CEFCD 164).

Chapter Eleven

Johnny Doran—Last of the Travelling Pipers

"A Piper in our street today
sat up and tuned and started to play,
and away, away, away on the tide,
for the music, it started on every side.
Doors and windows were open wide
and men left down their work and came,
and women with petticoats coloured like flame
and bare little feet that were blue with the cold
went dancing back to the age of the gold.
And all the world went gay, went gay,
for half an hour in our street today."
The Piper, Seumas O'Sullivan, 1879–1958

"Behold me now,
　　　　with my back to the wall,
playing music
　　　to empty pockets"
　　　　　　　Raftery, the Poet, nineteenth century

A gentleman piper, some wag somewhere once said, is somebody who can play the pipes, but doesn't. Whoever he was, we can assume he had little love for the skirl of one of the oldest, and certainly the most complex, wind-instrument in the world. His barbed wit may, of course, have been aimed at the Scottish or Irish bagpipe—the píob mór or war pipes—and not the uilleann pipes. The Scottish bagpipe and its Irish cousin, the píob mór, are mouth-blown instruments and are best heard out of doors as part of a marching band. The uilleann (elbow) pipes, as its name suggests, is a complex elbow-blown instrument comprising bag and chanter, drones and regulators (which provide chordal rhythm accompaniment), is played while seated with the drones lying across the right or left thigh and is best appreciated as a solo instrument or with fiddles or flutes. It is also an instrument which is best heard indoors, preferably in smoky back-rooms of late-night pubs or in old stone-floored country kitchens in front of open turf fires to fully capture the richness, the fullness of its three-octave range and the fine quality of tone of this truly unique and magnificent instrument, whose ancestry can be traced back to the eleventh century.

I first heard the uilleann pipes being played in the flesh by Seán Reid, a well known piper, originally from County Monaghan who lived in east Clare, at the Ennis Fleadh Cheoil of 1956. But the man who really turned me on to the instrument was the great west Clare piper, the late Willie Clancy. I will never forget, for as long as I live, that winter's night in the late Sixties when I fell under the spell of Willie's uilleann pipes in the back bar of Friel's pub in Miltown Malbay. From that moment on, I have harboured a burning passion for the uilleann pipes and piping. That's the thing about the pipes, you either love them or loathe them; you can never be noncommittal about them. But be warned, once captivated by them you will forever be held in their thrall.

Both Séamus Ennis and Willie Clancy's influence on pipes and piping over the last three decades have been enormous. Since Willie's untimely death in 1974, his home town of Miltown Malbay has played host to the annual

Willie Clancy Summer School, where hundreds of musicians converge on the town to learn and to play. And everywhere, of course, there are uilleann pipers, young and old, to be heard endlessly talking about, and endlessly playing, this captivating instrument.

The activities of the Willie Clancy Summer School are a far cry from the days when Johnny Doran, the last of the great travelling pipers, traversed the highways and byways in the Thirties and Forties, playing for crossroad dances, wakes and weddings, soirees, functions and village fairs. In pre-Famine Clare, the uilleann pipes had been a hugely popular instrument, most of which were made by the Moloney Brothers from Kilrush—Thomas, a blacksmith, and Andrew, a carpenter. An example of their work can be seen in the National Museum, one of the finest masterpieces in the uilleann pipe family. (Willie Clancy played a Moloney chanter, which can be heard on his recordings.) Three nineteenth-century Clare pipers of note were the legendary blind piper Garret Barry, born near Inagh in 1847 (regarded by many as a father figure of Clare music), Patrick Galvin, a native of Corrofin who emigrated to New Zealand in the post-Famine exodus, and Johnny Patterson, born near Feakle in east Clare and who emigrated to America, where he became a famous clown, ballad-writer and piper, touring the East Coast cities with various circus troupes. (We can only imagine the sound Patterson made as he sat playing his uilleann pipes in the centre ring, accompanied by an entire circus brass band!) By the turn of the century—Garret Barry had died in 1899—there were few pipers to be seen or heard anywhere in the county. It is difficult to find any references to piping in Clare between 1900 and the early Thirties, when Johnny Doran, then in his early twenties, first visited the county along with his brother Felix, who was also an uilleann piper of extraordinary talent.

Notes from the Heart

The sight and sound of Johnny Doran playing his pipes on the streets of a village in Clare in the Thirties must have been both exotic and exciting to all who witnessed it. He was a small, wiry, good-looking man with dark skin and black hair. According to the fiddler John Kelly, "He looked for all the world like an Indian." The few photos of Johnny still extant—swarthy, black-haired, with high cheekbones, intelligent eyes—would seem to confirm John Kelly's description of him.

Apart from his music, which put bread on his table during the summer months, Johnny bought and sold ponies and horses from and to farmers he encountered as he travelled the countryside. It is said by some that he did not drink, would never play his pipes past midnight and would often go into the fields after dark to play a tune for the little people. Wherever lies the truth, it was said of Johnny Doran that as both man and musician, you could meet no better. Wherever he played, Doran's piping weaved a magical web which both seduced and mesmerised the listener. For greater impact, he usually played in a standing position, his pipes, stock and drones resting across his right leg, which in turn rested on a make-shift leg-rest. Countless traditional musicians and lovers of traditional music, including some youthful pipers-to-be, Willie Clancy and Martin Talty who lived in west Clare and Martin Rochford and Seán Reid who lived in east Clare, were to fall under his spell. In recent years, Johnny Doran's music has become more influential than ever it was in his own lifetime, mainly due to the piping of such present-day virtuosi and exponents of Doran's style, ex-Bothy Band piper Paddy Keenan, the late John Keenan (Paddy's father), Finbar Furey, ex-Moving Hearts piper, Davy Spillane and Martin Nolan, a young Dublin piper now living in Ennistymon in County Clare.

Johnny Doran was born in 1907 into a family of

professional travelling musicians, and was a descendant of the legendary nineteenth-century Wicklow piper, John Cash. He, and his younger brother Felix, grew up in an atmosphere where the art of uilleann piping took precedence over all else. Johnny was to quickly prove to be an able and talented student, and very soon he was a fully-fledged uilleann piper carrying on a family tradition that stretched back through several generations. Later, in 1932, Johnny was to teach his younger brother, Felix, to play the pipes. Around the same time, Johnny took to the road and from then until his tragic death at the age of forty-two in 1950—the result of a wall falling on him while his caravan was parked near Christchurch in Dublin— Johnny Doran's pipes could be heard wherever there was a large gathering of people, be it a fair, crossroads-dance or a football match. Though he travelled widely, County Clare was to become his favourite stamping ground, attracted by the wealth of tradition still alive in the county and the fact that he found there a ready and deeply appreciative listening audience for his music. Johnny's brother Felix, also an accomplished uilleann piper, found in Clare, as Johnny did, a ready audience for his piping and visited the county as often as he could. It was from Felix that Willie Clancy purchased his first practice set of pipes. There was much celebration whenever Johnny Doran and his pipes arrived in a village or townland. As with the legendary eighteenth-century blind harper, O'Carolan, many families considered it a real honour to have Johnny Doran visit or play in their houses. His arrival in the village-square or the farmyard usually meant a time of festivity and celebration and some time off from the drudgery of everyday toil.

With the lengthening of the days and coming of the hawthorn blossom and the mayfly, Johnny Doran's gaily-coloured horse-drawn caravan could be seen drifting lazily towards a sheep or cattle-fair in Ennistymon or Kilrush or a wedding or house-dance in Miltown Malbay or Quilty. Though the war years greatly restricted his rural ramblings, he resumed his travelling in 1945 and from then until his death in 1950, Johnny Doran and his pipes were to be seen and heard in Galway, Mayo, Sligo, Cavan, Longford, Kildare, Wicklow, Wexford and, of course, his beloved Clare.

Johnny Doran's piping style was as wild and exciting as it was technically brilliant. He was, in the words of one writer, "A man of tremendous personal charisma and capable of sending out a musical pulse which utterly captivated the listener." Indeed, all who have heard Johhny Doran in the flesh speak of falling into a kind of rapture on hearing his headlong rush of bewitching music.

There's a story told of a man from the Feakle area in east Clare, so besotted by the uilleann pipes, and in particular with the piping of Johnny Doran, that he almost became an outcast in his own home in the mid-Forties. It seems that the man's wife was about to give birth, and on her going into the late stages of labour, he was dispatched that evening to the nearest village—five or six miles away—to summon the midwife. Speeding along on his bicycle, he espied a familiar horse-drawn caravan parked in a lay-by. He knew the caravan well—it was that of his musical hero, Johnny Doran. He wheeled the bike in to bid the time of day, only to find Johnny tuning his uilleann pipes. In that instant, all else was forgotten—his home, his family, his wife in the last stages of labour and probably even his own name as he slipped into the otherworld of tunes and names of tunes and players of tunes and the deadly spell of the drones and chanter. Only when he emerged from Johnny's caravan early the following morning to witness the soft dawn breaking did he recall his mission of the previous evening. We can only speculate about the reception the man received on arriving home. One teller of the tale (who swore it to be true) added that his infant son had a full set of teeth when the man finally got home. Such was the spellbinding power of Johnny Doran's piping.

Johnny Doran's repertoire of airs and dance tunes, all of which were well-known pieces, were played legato, with the open style of piping, for greater effect out of doors and in order to attract listeners, who would be moved to contribute a few pence. More than once, it is said, did a ten-shilling note (50 new pence)—an enormous sum in the Forties—find its way into Johnny's collection-box, contributed by music-loving farmers who could ill-afford such generous sums. He usually played the pipes in a standing position, with the drones laid across his right thigh, which rested on a T-shaped leg-rest. At a fair or football match, when Johnny had exhausted one patch, he moved on to another to blow up again his bag and chanter and fill the air with his extraordinary piping. Moving among a people suffering widespread economic hardships, Johnny Doran's music-making (along with indulging in a little horse-trading on the side) earned him a more than decent living.

Had it not been for the foresight of the late west Clare fiddler and concertina player John Kelly, then living in Dublin, we may not have had an opportunity to hear and appreciate Johnny Doran's unique piping style and stunning virtuosity. John Kelly first encountered Johnny Doran and his spellbinding piping at the fair of Kilkee in September 1932. John remembered this wiry, impish, dark-haired man driving the crowds who gathered round him wild with excitement. From then until Johnny's death in 1950, both men remained firm friends, often playing together at sessions. It was John Kelly who eventually persuaded Kevin Danaher of the Irish Folklore Commission of the necessity of committing Doran's piping to tape. The recordings were duly made in the Folklore Commission offices off St Stephen's Green, Dublin, in November 1946. John Kelly later recalled having a premonition that if Doran (who, at that time, was not in good health) was not recorded then he would never be. John's premonitions were to be proved correct. On or about New Year's Day in 1948, as Johnny was about to emerge from his caravan—which he had parked overnight by a high wall in a back lane opposite Christchurch Cathedral in Dublin—a fierce storm blew the wall onto his caravan, pinning Johnny underneath. He was dragged from beneath the rubble and taken to the Meath Hospital, suffering from injuries to his head, back and stomach. He survived the accident, but was to remain crippled from the waist down. Though he rallied somewhat and indeed travelled with his wife to his beloved Wicklow, his health deteriorated rapidly. He was re-admitted to St Vincent's Hospital in Athy, County Kildare where he died on 19 January 1950. Johnny Doran, last of the travelling pipers, was only forty years of age.

The Doran recordings, twenty in all, were held in the sound archive of the Department of Irish Folklore, UCD, and did not see the light of day, apart from the odd outing on radio, until 1988, when a complete collection of his recorded works was released on cassette. (*The Bunch of Keys—The Complete Recordings of Johnny Doran*. Issued by Comhairle Bhéaloideas Éireann, CBE 001). Though Johnny himself was in poor health at the time of the recordings, they show a man utterly at one with his instrument and his music. Towards the end, as the great virtuoso lay in his hospital bed, he would be visited by his good Clare musician friends John Kelly, Willie Clancy and Seán Reid. The topic of the bedside conversation was invariably music. Johnny's pipes would be taken out of the case, and though he was in considerable pain, Johnny would prop himself up in bed and play his still-wild music on the chanter, while John Kelly or Seán Reid would blow the bellows and Willie Clancy would play the regulators. Indeed the last tune he ever played was on Willie Clancy's chanter.

The great collector and historian Breandán Breathnach said of him, "It always strikes me that Johnny was playing for himself, in response to some inner urge or feeling and that he went over and over the tune until he got the whole thing out of his system. He had a total mastery of the chanter and regulators."

To appreciate this total control and musicality, one has only to listen to Johnny's rendering of *Rakish Paddy*, which captivated the ear and imagination of Seán Ó Riada and Willie Clancy among others. If these recordings represent Johnny Doran's piping while not in good shape physically, we can only imagine how awesome his technique must have been when at his peak in the Thirties and early Forties. His repertoire included a selection of reels, jigs, hornpipes and airs which Johnny learned as a boy in his native Wicklow. Many old Clare musicians referred to these tunes as travellers' tunes (such as *The Blackbird, An Chúileann* (or Coolin), *Colonel Fraser, The Fox Hunt* or *The High Level Hornpipe*), indicating that these tunes were associated with professional travelling musicians such as Johnny, his brother Felix or the Dunne brothers (a family of travelling musicians from County Limerick). Among these were the big reels such as *Rakish Paddy, Colonel Fraser, My Love is in America* and *Miss McLeod's Reel*. Favourite jigs included *Coppers and Brass* (also known as *The Humours of Ennistymon*) and *The Rambling Pitchfork. The Coolin* would have been one of Johnny's favourite slow airs. Though he never recorded it, the great descriptive piece *The Fox Hunt* (recorded by his brother Felix in the Sixties) would also have been one of his virtuoso showpieces. Listening now to Johnny's rendering of these recorded pieces gives us an idea of the tunes which obviously held his interest. Though he must have played the tunes countless times down the years, his fascination with the inner nature of the tunes, and the excitement he exudes through his execution of them, is fairly palpable. He never would play the tune the same way twice, and *Rakish Paddy, Colonel Fraser, McLeod's* and *The High Level Hornpipe* were among his crowd-pullers and show-stoppers. As evident in his recordings of the above tunes, Johnny would play the tune over and over, exploring new possibilities in a flurry of both intricate legato (open fingering) and staccato (close fingering) runs, probing every hidden nook and cranny of the tune, probing and teasing out the delicate nuances and musical shadings, pushing—indeed often seemingly testing—his own ability to breathe new life and energy into the oft-played pieces. To highlight a certain part of a tune and create dramatic tension, he would, for effect on the third or fourth time around, switch off his drones and regulators. This was to let the chanter speak on its own and to demonstrate his dazzling mix of legato and staccato fingerwork. The drones would then be switched back on, followed by his equally dazzling regulator playing. A good example of this technique can be heard in his rendition of the double-jig *Coppers and Brass* and *Miss McLeod's Reel* (obviously two of his big tunes). Here, as he brings the tune to a climax of fiery fingerwork on the chanter, he switches on the drones and then employs an accompaniment of syncopated regulator harmony-chording to stunning effect. In Doran's piping, we can detect a controlled wildness—a fiery passion—to his playing that reeks of the wild places and the open road travelled, the tumult of country fairs, the gaiety of the crossroads dance, the campfire at night and dewy bird-loud dawns. We can also detect something far older, deeper and mysterious: an ancient voice speaking of a long-dead people from a forgotten place and age.

PJ Curtis

Listening in this age to Johnny Doran's piping, we hear a supreme musician at work. We also hear the sound of the last century and indeed further back, to perhaps Romany and Gypsy travellers who carried their music from India to Europe, some of which no doubt lodged, and may still be detected, in the furthermost inhabited islands on the edge of the European land-mass. Most of all we hear the spirit of a man, whose life was lived out on the quiet country roads, in the noisy, bustling rural villages and among the Plain People of Ireland and whose wild uilleann pipe playing of the old reels, jigs, hornpipes and slow airs touched the hearts and souls of all who heard him. Though that spirit lives on through the piping of Paddy Keenan, Finbar Furey and Davy Spillane, the environment which nourished that spirit and gave the music its essence, energy but most of all its grand beauty, is disappearing fast. The days of Johnny Doran and the travelling pipers are gone for ever (Johnny lies buried with his own people in Rathnew, County Wicklow, as does his piper brother Felix who died in 1973), but his music—wild, passionate and free—is, thankfully, still with us.

In the meantime, I recommend that you take the odd sip from, as one poet described the uilleann pipes, those hives of honeyed sound, and prepare to be both bewitched and enthralled. It will do your heart and soul a power of good. It certainly does for me, every time I hear that eloquent, beautiful language as spoken by the drones, bag and chanter.

Discography:

The Bunch of Keys—The Complete Recordings of Johnny Doran (Comhairle Bhéaloideas Éireann, CBE 001 Cass. only).

Chapter Twelve

Doolin—Traditional Music Mecca

Time was when the Road To Lisdoonvarna was the name of a well-known reel and the road to Doolin was populated only by the local inhabitants going about their everyday work or returning from visits from nearby towns and villages. Times have changed, and these days the road to Doolin is a familiar road to the hitchers and hikers and other assorted visitors who make regular pilgrimages to the tiny fishing village situated six miles north-west of the spa town of Lisdoonvarna in north Clare. The thousands who descend on Doolin annually are lured not only by the extraordinary land and seascapes but also to experience, first-hand, the magic of sitting in, or indeed outside, any one of the village's three pubs and witnessing a session of traditional music in full spate. These days there are music sessions to be heard in Doolin almost any hour of the day or night, winter or summer, as fiddlers from Sweden or Brittany trade tunes with local fiddlers, flute players or pipers. And so it has been since Doolin was discovered to have at its core an untapped vein of folk culture at its purest. Word of this find got out and within a short time this previously quiet fishing hamlet hummed to the sound of visitors from all over Ireland and later the Continent, in search of what Doolin offered in abundance—an authentic living culture of traditional music and song.

Those early waves of visitors made directly for Fisher

Street and O'Connor's Pub, whose owners Gus and Doll gave all comers an old-world, homely welcome offered with great charm and genuine hospitality. The O'Connor family are one of the oldest in Doolin, and Gus O'Connor's great-great-grandfather obtained a pub licence in 1832. Throughout the nineteenth and twentieth centuries, for one hundred and sixty years, the O'Connor family played genial host to locals and travellers from far and wide. The pub is now run by Susan O'Connor, who proudly lays claim to being the fifth generation O'Connor to inhabit the establishment. From as early as the middle of the last century, Doolin offered to all a non-judgemental environment, a free-and-easy, come-day-go-day, left-bank retreat, in sharp contrast to the rather staid Victorian ambience of the nearby spa town, Lisdoonvarna.

In the 1920s and 30s, Doolin had been discovered by the bohemian set. Artists and writers such as George Bernard Shaw, JM Synge, Augustus John, Dylan Thomas and Oliver St John Gogarty spent idyllic summers in and around this sleepy fishing-village, mostly in the convivial, welcoming atmosphere always on tap at the O'Connor hostelry. Indeed, it could be said that the genuine, open-hearted welcome proffered to countless visitors by the O'Connor family down the years lies at the centre of the magic that is associated with Doolin. Today, that welcoming aura is still the initial, engaging atmosphere sensed by the visitor. Added to this welcome are the seemingly endless music sessions to further engage and bewitch the first-timer. A visit to Doolin was to step through a portal to a world which seemed to exist in a very separate dimension. It was as though one had stepped back into another age; a strange timeless place where only the celebration of the moment matters. In this rarefied atmosphere, as the tunes, the songs and the stories wove their magic spell, the real world of cares, worries and responsibilities slipped further and further away. Many who visited Doolin in those early days were so bewitched by the village and its lifestyle that they set up home there to become Dooliners—fully fledged locals in every sense of the word.

Doolin, once a quiet fishing village tucked away on the north-west coast of Clare, has over the last two decades at least become a veritable mecca for fans of traditional music from all over the world and has established for itself an international reputation unequalled anywhere on this island. Indeed, it might be said that Doolin is to Irish traditional music what New Orleans is to traditional jazz, the important difference being that Doolin still remains relatively unsullied and untainted by over-commercialisation and gross exploitation. In the mid-Forties, when the pre-eminent uilleann piper and collector Séamus Ennis travelled to Doolin to collect the music and song of the locality, he found it to be a vigorous centre of music and dance. At that period it certainly was still very much the hub of the vanishing Clare Gaeltacht, a fact that interested Séamus Ennis greatly. Here he knew he would witness and collect folk stories, songs, poetry and music, entirely unblemished by any outside influence, which had been handed down intact from generation to generation.

While in Doolin in September 1945 Séamus first came into contact with a twenty-four-year-old whistle-player who captured his attention and his keen ear. This was Séamus Ennis's first meeting with Pakie Russell, who later became better known as a fine concertina player, folk-storyteller and able spinner of his own tall and humorous tales. Another local Doolin musician to be recorded by Séamus on that visit was fiddler, concertina player and singer, Paddy Killourhy. At a recording session at Gus and Dolly O'Connor's pub, Paddy gave Séamus *Cathaoir an Phíobaire* (*The Piper's Chair*), now a well-known jig.

PJ Curtis

The Radió Éireann (RTE) broadcaster, Ciarán Mac Mathúna, also made many collecting trips to Doolin throughout the Fifties and his field recordings of the music and song of the area were aired on his ground-breaking *Ceolta Tíre* and *A Job of Journeywork* on Radió Éireann. When the poet Michael Cody visited Doolin in the Sixties he was totally captivated by the old-world atmosphere which still existed there. He too was also utterly enthralled by the wealth of music, story and song he encountered. Cody later wrote that in Doolin he discovered "...a place where real folk musicians played music which was a living thing and not something dead for centuries and artificially resurrected by scholarly types who met in very self-conscious folk-clubs at weekends."

In the Seventies and Eighties, as the word spread about Doolin, more and more musicians, not to mention listeners, travelled there to meet, play and enjoy the casual yet friendly, convivial atmosphere. To drop into O'Connor's, McDermott's or McGann's Pub, run by Tony and Tommy McGann, was to chance on an impromptu session storming away for hours and perhaps consisting of some of the finest traditional musicians to be heard anywhere. At any given time, winter or summer, day or night, it was possible to sit in a cosy corner and witness the music of Tommy Peoples, Noel Hill, Tony Linnane, Christy Barry, brothers Michael and Séamus Hynes, Paddy and John Killourhy, Davy Spillane, Matt Molloy, Frankie Gavin, Paddy Keenan, Sharon Shannon, Mary Custy or Kevin Griffin playing in different combinations.

No visit to Doolin was complete, however, without hearing one of the legendary Russell brothers, Micho, Gus or Pakie. All three brothers inherited the great store of local music and folklore, which stretched back perhaps a thousand years. The tradition and spirit which the Russell brothers represented was the reason musicians and international visitors were drawn to the area in the first place, a fine, delicate spirit which still permeates the musical atmosphere of Doolin. Over the last three decades Micho, the more famous of the trio, took his vast repertoire of traditional music, story and songs to the world by recording several albums, television and radio appearances, publishing collections of these stories, songs and tunes, embarking on regular tours of Europe and the United States to become somewhat of a traditional music superstar. Amidst all this activity, he could still find time to sit quietly in one of the Doolin pubs, charming listeners with his hypnotic tin whistle or generally discussing any aspect of his music with anyone who approached him. Micho's brothers Gus and Pakie were, in Michael Cody's words, "...happy to stay in Doolin and let the world come to them." Which indeed it did in numbers so great that a hostel, a Doolin-Deli and three restaurants quickly sprang up to deal with the increased volume of visitors. When the writer Hugo Hamilton visited the village in the summer of 1993, he found a very different Doolin than did Dylan Thomas or JM Synge several decades ago. Hamilton observed, "All species of traveller co-existed comfortably; backpackers, bandanas and bikers, Moto Guzzi and MCP Les Corbeaux emblazoned on their jackets." He also saw the inherent dangers in this growing influx of visitors. "The danger now is tourism fatigue, not towards Germans or Australians, but the noisy Irish hordes who arrive on the weekends with their own homogeneous craic, singing Beatles songs in the beer-garden across the road from O'Connor's Pub."

But the magic of Doolin remains unique and special in a way that transcends even the music to be heard there. The Doolin that Michael Cody and several other writers have described has altered greatly over the last three decades. The huge influx of visitors each summer has seen to that. Gone is the changeless, Brigadoon-like atmosphere and way of life which pertained in the village until the mid to late Seventies. There is an International Hostel now in Doolin, complete with bureau de change, which houses visitors from as far away as Hamburg or Honolulu. The Fisher Street of today is a far cry from the Fisher Street of even twenty years ago, with its craft shop, delicatessen, record shop and restaurants. But apart from the dreamy, otherworld atmosphere which hangs over the village, it is the inhabitants, the pubs and the music which still attract pilgrims from every corner of the globe A visit to any of the three music pubs in the village, O'Connor's, McGann's or McDermott's, may now often seem like stepping into some great pan-European gathering. Swedes rub shoulders with Italians, Germans with Bretons and Australians with Americans. It is not uncommon to catch sight of foreign hitchers on the roads out of Dublin carrying cards with the word "Doolin" written on them.

In recent years it has become perhaps a little more difficult to witness the calibre of spontaneous music-session once common in Doolin. The sheer number of visitors, coupled with the number of often over-enthusiastic fiddlers and whistle-players—keen to join in the session and the craic—caused many local musicians to seek less congested havens to play their music. "The place has changed," complained one musician who frequented Doolin in the Sixties and Seventies "that was the golden age of Doolin, when the Russell brothers, all three of them...and Killourhy brothers could be heard in O'Connor's Pub any evening, playing, singing, telling stories and talking to genuinely interested people. Now you have Americans or Australians coming to Doolin to listen to Germans or Dutch play Irish music! Many of the people who come these days, don't really know why they're there or even what theyre looking for."

Nevertheless the village still attracts musicians and ordinary visitors from all corners and manages to retain its own unique new-age bohemian ambience. There still exists in Doolin a healthy sense of community, a vital, secure community which still exudes hospitality and friendliness. Moreover, though the very real danger exists of the emergence of an international, homogenised Doolin, the village still offers a wholeness, a totality of old-world culture that has been lost, discarded or ignored elsewhere in Irish society. One visitor from Alabama said of his visit to Doolin, "I never wanted to leave the place. The friendliness, the music...the fact that the rat-race has by-passed the place...the strange, magic light at dawn and dusk.... It has that certain spirit in the air." This, then, is part of the unique attraction of Doolin. If it is over-exploited or tampered with in an insensitive way, it may yet destroy that spirit, that special magic that lies at the heart of Doolin's appeal.

Discography:

The Russell Family of Doolin, County Clare/The Russell family (Topic 12T251).
The Man From Clare/Micho Russell(GTD).
The Limestone Rock/Micho Russell (GTD).
Traditional Music of County Clare/Various (Free Reed FRR 004).
Trip to Doolin/Kevin Griffin.
The Stonemason/Various Artists.

Chapter Thirteen

Tony Linnane—Born to the Music

"I'll play you jigs, and Maurice Kean,
Where nets are laid to dry,
I've silken strings would draw a dance
From girls are lame or shy;
Four strings I've brought from Spain and France
To make your long men skip and prance,
Till stars look out to see the dance
Where nets are laid to dry."
Beg-Innish, JM Synge

In a county which boasts so many active traditional musicians, it is perfectly natural that a great many young people should develop an interest in, or show a flair for, one of the principal traditional music instruments. In most Clare musical houses, these would include tin whistle, flute, concertina or fiddle. Indeed it is generally expected that in a household where traditional music is played by one or more parent, the art will be passed on to one or more of the children. When a teenager in such a household takes to playing the fiddle, accordion or whistle, it is considered fairly normal. It is exciting, too, to witness youngsters, particularly those between the ages of eight and twelve, exhibit early prodigious talent on a particular instrument. But what of a child, not yet of school-going age, who shows such exceptional musical talent before the age of four as to leave all who witness it scrambling for an explanation for the phenomenon? So it was for Pat and Mary Linnane of Corrofin in north Clare, when in 1960, Tony, the youngest of their two boys, astounded and stunned his parents by picking up a harmonica and without very much ado proceeding to play a reel after very little practice and absolutely no tuition. Young Tony was barely three years of age. His mother, Mary, recalls, "There was a harmonica lying around the house at the time and one day Tony picked it up and within a few minutes he was playing a tune. We were absolutely amazed. Nobody in the house played the harmonica. Pat (his father) was actually frightened. He'd never seen or heard of anyone so young playing like that. He was able to bring out tunes before he could talk. He just seemed to get the music from out of the air." Within a short time Tony's repertoire had grown to include many fairly difficult reels, jigs and hornpipes. It was quite clear to all who witnessed him play that his ability on the harmonica far exceeded that of an adult player with many years of practice behind them. It was also obvious to all who heard Tony at that period (as did this writer in 1962/3) that here was a musical prodigy of rare and exceptional talent; a talent which was to be both treasured and nurtured. Too often we hear of youngsters who show prodigious talents at a very early stage, only to witness that talent fade or mysteriously dry up when they approach adolescence. Three decades later, Tony Linnane's musical abilities continue to thrill, astound and enthral the listener. One thing is different, however: Tony no longer plays the harmonica, the instrument he mastered at the tender age of three. For well over twenty years now, Tony Linnane has been a fiddle player of both talent and renown whose considerable reputation and influence is known and acclaimed wherever Irish traditional fiddle playing is appreciated.

The first, and perhaps the most important, influence on Tony Linnane's musical development was his father, Pat. Though he was a reluctant and private whistle player, Pat Linnane is still fondly remembered as a man with a big heart who harboured within that heart an all-consuming passion which shaped and enriched his entire life, while touching everyone who came in contact with him. That passion was for Irish traditional music. So much so, in fact, that other local musicians regularly consulted him about tunes or learned new tunes directly from his vast repertoire, which Pat carried in his head. In his youth, before radio and record players and while working in other parts of Clare as a builder-contractor, Pat would come into regular contact with other Clare or Galway musicians. He would then learn any new tunes from them and on his return to Corrofin, he would then whistle, note for note, the newly acquired tune for other musicians, including members of the Kilfenora Céilí Band, who would hastily learn them and include them in their repertoires. The late Jimmy Ward recalled the excitement of the prospect of a new tune which might be carried back by Pat from Tulla in east Clare or from the Loop Head peninsula in south-west Clare. Thus, tunes and styles, like musical pollen or spores, were transmitted from one area to another. Without doubt, Pat Linnane played a crucial part in that process of cross-fertilisation.

There is no doubt that from the moment Tony Linnane, and his older brother Seán, also a talented musician, were born (and indeed before they were born), they both consciously and subconsciously absorbed the music that was to be heard almost continuously in the Linnane household. It was said that a musician would not pass the Linnane door, day or night, without dropping in for the chat, the tea and the few tunes. It was in this vibrant social and musical atmosphere that Tony developed from a child-prodigy harmonica-player to teenage fiddle virtuoso. His initial interest in the fiddle came about from hearing a well-known Kilfenora player who both encouraged and influenced him. "It was in 1970," Tony recalls. "I was about thirteen and PJ Lynch, the fiddle-player with the Kilfenora Band, was staying in our house for a few weeks; he was working with my father at the time. He would play most evenings and I just loved his music. When I would come home from school, I'd pick up his fiddle and try the scale and later try and bring a tune out. I think *Lucy Cambell's* was the first reel I attempted. That was my first encounter with the fiddle." Following this initial introduction to the instrument, it was decided that Tony should get a fiddle and attend fiddle classes.

The obvious choice for music teacher was music master Frank Custy, who lived in the nearby village of Toonagh. It was under Frank's committed tutelage that Tony quickly developed his playing and his music reading skills. Frank remembers meeting the shy young Corrofin boy for the first time: "I think he had only one…maybe two tunes when he first came to me. But straight away, I could see that he had great ability—natural talent to burn!" It was at one of those classes that he was to meet the musician with whom he was to form a fruitful, long-term and most rewarding musical association. "It was in Toonagh at one of Frank's classes that I met and played with Noel Hill for the first time. We were about the same age and we struck it off from the start." His next significant musical encounter came about one night in the Christmas of 1971. "My mother woke me from sleep very late one night to tell me there was a great fiddle player downstairs." It was none other than Tommy Peoples. Tony's father, Pat, had spotted a hitch-hiker with a fiddle-case tucked under his arm and, never one for passing up the opportunity of meeting a new musician, he offered the stranger a lift from Ennis to Corrofin. Not surprisingly, the hitch-hiker-musician found himself in Linnane's kitchen enthralling all with his electrifying fiddle playing, including the now wide-awake fourteen-year-old Tony, who sat enraptured until the early hours of the morning. It was the first of many such nights in the company of this fiddle-playing wizard from Saint Johnston in County Donegal. "I was amazed by Tommy. It was so different for me to hear playing and music like this. I had heard other great fiddle players, Seán Keane of The Chieftains who once visited the house or Brendan McGlinchey and Séamus Connolly on the radio, but I'd never heard playing like this in the flesh before." Hearing and actually seeing Tommy play had a profound effect on Tony's own musical development. Tommy became a regular visitor to the Linnane home and Tony quickly absorbed new tunes, ideas and perhaps most importantly, new fiddle techniques. He is quick to acknowledge his debt to Tommy's early influence, encouragement and guidance, especially when it came to developing technique and personal style. "I can thank him for teaching me ornamentation; I'd been used to playing in a Clare style which is a more rhythmic approach, mainly for dancing. It was wonderful to be exposed to Tommy's Donegal fiddle style, with its emphasis on ornamentation—the rolls, grace-notes, bowing and so forth." Tony's repertoire was to be greatly expanded by Tommy's great wealth of northern tunes, most of them unknown in Clare. *The Oak Tree* was one of the big reels which Tommy taught to Tony, a tune which has continued to fascinate him down the years, no matter how many times he plays it. He was in his twenties before he recognised a personal fiddle-style emerging. "My fiddle playing in my teens was by and large influenced by players like Tommy and so it was until the late Seventies when I grew into my own style, so to speak." Tony's playing had indeed reached a stage of maturity that is rarely found in a musician still barely out of his teens. The fluid, confident musical flow and drive, the delicacy and complex subtleties of his ornamentation and graceful bowing technique had all fully developed, giving him his unique and highly distinctive fiddle style, which he retains and employs to the full to this day.

By 1974 Tommy Peoples had moved to Dublin to join The Bothy Band, and Tony, now sixteen, could be found more and more in the company of his new musical partner and fellow Clareman, the young virtuoso concertina player Noel Hill and coming into contact with other fine young fiddlers such as Frankie Gavin from Galway and James Kelly and Paddy Glackin from Dublin city. But is was the highly-charged musical chemistry at work between Tony and Noel's fiddle and concertina which was to become the talk of the traditional music fraternity. Their maturity of style, their freshness and vitality of sound, their stunning virtuosity and their absolute musical rapport earned them acclaim far beyond the local and county boundaries. This fame eventually led to the recording of one of the great albums of the Seventies. The album, simply titled *Noel Hill and Tony Linnane* (Tara Records), set new standards and earned the players recognition and new fans the world over. If any had doubts that recorded traditional music in its purest form was in any danger, these doubts were dispelled with the release of this now classic tour-de-force album. It was obvious to all who had ears to listen and the heart to know that here was Clare fiddle and concertina music of the highest order, played by two young virtuosi at the height of their musical prowess.

As outlined in the Noel Hill profile, their professional relationship was to last for several years, seeing them through tours at home and abroad, guest-starring on albums by Planxty and Christy Moore and even forming the short-lived group Inchiquin, with banjo-player Kieran Hanrahan and singer-guitarist Tony Callanan. This group lasted but a year or so, when Hanrahan and Callanan departed to form the group Stockton's Wing, leaving Tony and Noel Hill to continue as a duo. This situation did not duly bother the pair. "Actually, we were happier playing in a more traditional context and this we did and continued to do until I decided to quit the life of a full-time musician. I had been seven years playing as a professional musician and I felt I had enough of the road. Noel decided to carry on alone and I came back to Clare to a regular job and playing for enjoyment only at weekends and other informal sessions."

Since then Tony has married and settled down in Ennis. But music and the social life that surrounds the music scene is never far away. "There are always musicians dropping by and there are regular sessions here and there to go to. I could get rusty but I never do. I play now for enjoyment and for the sake of the music." So what excites his musical taste-buds these days? "Well, I love playing with flute players. I love the sound of fiddle and flute together and to play with people like Eamonn Cotter, Jim O'Donoghue, Kevin Crawford or Matt Molloy is my idea of a good session." Does he listen to other kinds of music? "I love American acoustic music, Doc Watson and the like, Ry Cooder too, but I listen mainly to Irish traditional. That's what I am, after all, a traditional musician."

A quiet and shy man in his mid-thirties, Tony Linnane is and has been, since he amazed his parents at the age of three with his early showing of musical promise, a gifted traditional fiddle player of exceptional skill, finesse and fluency of expression. These days he plays for all who will listen when the spirit moves him. He looks forward to any encounter with other local or visiting musicians, when he will settle in some quiet session, rosin the bow and enter into that very separate world of music, inhabited only by like-minded players and listeners. In that world, Tony Linnane is utterly at one with his instrument and his music, speaking his first and original language—that of music directly from the heart and soul.

Discography:

Noel Hill and Tony Linnane/Noel Hill and Tony Linnane (Tara 2006).
The Iron Behind the Velvet/Christy Moore (Tara 2002).
The Woman I Loved So Well/Planxty (Tara 3005).

Chapter Fourteen

Frank Custy—Passing the Torch

"There is only one way of becoming a traditional singer or player, and that is by listening to genuine material performed in a traditional manner."
Breandán Breathnach, *Folk Music and Dances of Ireland*

It is widely accepted that Clare produces more traditional musicians per capita than any other county. Given that fact, it comes as no surprise to find that there is at present a great number of teen and pre-teen traditional music practitioners to be found the length and breadth of the county. These days we are not surprised to daily learn of the emergence in this or that locality of some new and extremely talented young fiddle player, concertina player, accordion player or whistle player. Invariably, these young virtuosi are in their early teens and have usually acquired their art in a number of ways. Those born into households where traditional music is played may spend their formative years learning their craft at a parent's knee, while others take inspiration and are influenced by the great wealth of traditional music now available on commercial disc and from radio and television. A wide number of traditional music programmes are available on national and local radio. Ciarán Mac Mathúna, Peter Browne and Kieran Hanrahan present excellent regular programmes on RTE

Radio 1, while presenters Áine Hensey and Tim Dennehy showcase over fifteen hours of the best of traditional music and song per week in Áine's nightly *Mist-Covered Mountain* programme and Tim's Sunday evening programme on Clare (96.4) FM, the local Clare radio station. While there is obviously a great deal to be gained through the medium and influence of radio, in the end, as Breandán Breathnach suggests, the only sure way of learning traditional music is to witness the music being played in a live situation. Those lucky enough to be in an area to avail of the opportunity receive the precious gift from regular visits to a traditional music teacher.

One of the most renowned and respected teachers of traditional music active in the county is Toonagh man, Frank Custy. Encountering Frank, a schoolteacher by profession, is to encounter a big-hearted, warm and energetic middle-aged man whose enthusiasm, love of music, and particularly the teaching of music, is palpable. That enthusiasm and love for the music has communicated directly to hundreds of his music students since he first began to teach music back in the mid-Sixties. Some of County Clare's, and indeed Ireland's, best-known traditional musicians have passed through his weekly classes. Among those to benefit from Frank's committed tutelage have been Noel Hill, Tony Linnane, James Cullinan, Siobhán Peoples, Sharon Shannon and his own daughters Frances (who runs a music shop in Ennis and also teaches traditional music), Catherine, Mary and son Tola Custy.

Nobody is more surprised than Frank himself that he ended up teaching traditional music. "I grew up in a household that was fanatical about hurling. The hay could be left, as long we were involved in sport. There was no music in the house, although there was music in the previous generation. All my aunts played. The fiddle I now play belonged to my aunt." His introduction to traditional music came about gradually. "I grew up listening to the pop-music of the period and then rock n' roll, but the local dances we went to were all Irish music céilís—the Kilfenora and the Tulla Céilí Bands played fairly regularly—so I suppose I was being influenced without realising it." Frank's first real involvement with traditional music came when he returned in 1961 to Toonagh to take up a teaching post in the local national school. His co-teacher, Mrs Connolly, insisted that music be taught in the school. Utterly without any music or music-teaching skills, Frank wisely sought help and advice from the great piper Seán Reid. "I met Seán and he tried the impossible, to get me to both read and play music—all in the one night!" Seán Reid did give Frank one useful piece of advice—if he was serious about learning to play and read music, he should go to one of the best-known and one of the last of the full-time music teachers in Clare, Jack Mulkere. Frank immediately fell under the spell of this charismatic teacher and raconteur. "Jack fascinated me. His personality was so strong. He could hold a class spellbound with stories, folklore and of course all his tunes. He told a story about every tune—its background and history. The atmosphere in his classes was unbelievable." In this energised atmosphere, Frank progressed quickly, learning to read music and play banjo and fiddle. Before too long, he was passing on to the school pupils what Jack had passed to him. In very few years, the early fruits of his work could be seen, and heard, in the unusually high percentage of good young players emerging from his Toonagh music classes. Initially, Frank taught music through the staff notation, but later switched to his own letter system, which concentrated more on the student's ability to play by ear. Frank firmly believes that for the natural student-musicians, this system works best. Considering the speed at which his students, even the slower, less music-minded students progressed using the letter system, it has obviously proved successful over the years. Apart from the music-teaching work in his own locality, Frank was instrumental in setting up music classes in other areas throughout the county. "It was my job to match the venue with a teacher and get the first few nights going. It was a great experience for me to see what other people were doing—I learned a lot that way, particularly about how other teachers approach their work." A major turning point in his own music-teaching methods came about through some observations and constructive criticisms made to him by a schools music inspector Micheál Ó hEidhin.

"Micheál came one day to hear my musicians play and he should have been impressed, but he wasn't. In the class were fiddle players Bernie Whelan, James Cullinan and my own daughter Mary and they were as good as you would hear. After hearing them play he said, 'They all sound alike! They all sound like you!' I was taken aback at his comments; now I'm very grateful for what he told me that day." Ó hEidhin impressed on Frank the inherent dangers in producing sound-alike, cloned players, without individualism or personal style. Frank sees that advice, somewhat of a shock at at the time, as being the turning point of his music teaching career. From that moment on, he concentrated in allowing his students as much personal freedom and musical space as they needed to develop individual playing skills and style, to capture what he describes as "...that free spirit; the freedom to make the music they hear in their own heads." More than a few of Frank's pupils down the years have benefited from this generosity of attitude.

How does he feel about Fleadh Cheoil competitions? "I'm totally against the training of musicians just for competitions. It stifles their individuality. One of our best fiddle-players, James Cullinan, was crucified at several Fleadh competitions for his bowing. He was greatly upset.... I told him to ignore the judges and carry on and develop in his own way. He did and listen to him now...a wonderful player!" Frank also firmly believes that the essence of the music is related to set-dancing. "Good set-dancers make you feel good if you're playing for them. If the dancers are bad, the music probably won't be good either." He believes too that anyone can play, regardless of background, and quotes his own teacher Jack Mulkere. "Jack used to say, 'Everyone can type, though some can type better than others.' It's the same with music. Of course natural musical talent sets some musicians apart. Some can hear a tune once and have it for ever. It's to do with having a good musical memory." Among those of his pupils with natural talent in abundance would be included Sharon Shannon, Siobhán Peoples, Tony Linnane, Noel Hill, James Cullinan, Dermot Lernihan (of the group Fisher Street) and his own daughter Mary. "From the moment I heard them play, it was immediately obvious they had something extra. They had the golden touch. Noel Hill had a real traditional style, even when he had only a few tunes, and Dermot Lernihan was already a genius on the accordion at the age or five or so! Sharon Shannon had it as well. I have a two fiddle pupils at the moment, Michelle O'Brien and Yvonne Casey. Both have that special quality. I can take them so far, then if they really want to continue playing, they will move on to other teachers." For many years, it was only children and teenagers who came to learn music. Now he is happy too with the increasing number of adult students who regularly attend his classes. For some it can be an exciting adventure and a positive journey or self-discovery and self-renewal. Frank recounts one such example. "One middle-aged woman, from Ennistymon, had an accordion in the house that nobody played. She tried to sell it and when she couldn't, she decided to come to me to learn to play it. She's now one of my best pupils. She came on so fast, she even surprised herself! She will be able to join in any session in a year or two. She is now a much happier, more contented person than she used to be. Music makes you a happier person. It's therapeutic."

In his three decades of passing the torch, in communicating his knowledge, techniques and, more importantly perhaps, his love and feeling for the music, Frank Custy still maintains a positive, open-hearted and extremely giving approach to the teaching of music and to his young charges. "I've taught music to hundreds of kids since I begun back in the Sixties—the great, the good, the average and the bad. If only ten out of every hundred I teach play well, or even continue to play after they leave or grow older, I am happy!"

We live in a country which often pays national tribute to the trite, the transient and the transparent, while many of the real heroes and heroines go unsung, uncelebrated and unrewarded. Though he would scoff at the suggestion, Frank Custy, and the handful of music teachers like him, is, in more ways than one, heroic. Heroic in his unswerving and total commitment to his calling. Heroic in his ongoing love affair with both the music and the transmitting of that music and, more importantly perhaps, the love of traditional music to each and every starry-eyed pupil who turns up at one of his Friday night classes with a fiddle, tin-whistle or nothing more than a half-hearted desire to learn a jig, reel or hornpipe. There are rarely award ceremonies, monuments or citations offered to such devoted masters such as Frank Custy. Perhaps his real and lasting rewards are embodied in the persons and music of some of Clare's finest musicians: Sharon Shannon, Mary Custy, Siobhán Peoples, Noel Hill, Tony Linnane or James Cullinan. When Sharon, Noel or his own daughter Mary Custy next step on a concert stage in Dublin, London, New York or San Francisco, part of music master Frank Custy's generous musical heart and soul will be there with them. And that, surely, is monument enough for any teacher of Irish traditional music.

Chapter Fifteen

Paul Brock—Box of Delights

"My father played the melodeon
outside the garden gate;
There were stars in the morning east
And they danced to his music."
A Christmas Childhood, Patrick Kavanagh

It's probably fair to say that when it comes to nominating the most popular instrument among musicians in Irish traditional music down the years, at least in terms of numbers of practitioners, the accordion would probably win hands down. The instrument gained widespread acceptance in the 1950s, mainly due to the work of players such as the legendary Paddy O'Brien from Portroe in County Tipperary, Joe Derrane, born in Boston of Irish parents, and Joe Cooley from east Galway. There were, of course, other contributory factors, such as the work and influence of great Dublin traditional musician, Bill Harte and Sonny Brogan, who were already established players of both style and substance.

The 78 RPM recordings and radio broadcasts in the Fifties and Sixties of the great players, such as O'Brien and Cooley, served to establish the accordion as a dominant sound, particularly among ensemble players and céilí band musicians, who were no doubt attracted to its powerful resonance, drive and cutting edge. Throughout the country, instrument shops reported huge increases in the sales of two and three-row accordions. One had only to look in the window of any average instrument shop of the period to appreciate this upsurge in sales, usually reflected in the entire shop-window being given over to displaying the instrument. The two leading instrument shops in Dublin, Waltons of North Frederick Street, who sold the Paulo Soprani (the most popular model) and Walkers of Liffey Street, agents for Hohners, logged massive sales of accordions during the late Fifties and Sixties.

Of the hundreds of accordion players to emerge since the Fifties there have been only a handful who stand out from the crowd. Among those are Joe Burke, Ann Conroy, Máirtín O'Connor (Galway), Jackie Daly (Cork), Paddy O'Brien (Offaly), Séamus and Brendan Begley (Kerry), Dermot Byrne (Donegal), Tony MacMahon, Bobby Gardner, Andrew McMahon, PJ King and Conor Keane (Clare), each a consummate musician of exceptional taste and talent.

There are few traditional accordionists, however, who can lay claim to as varied a playing career as that of one of the most respected players in the country—Paul Brock. Still in his forties, Paul Brock's playing CV is hugely impressive. Acknowledged accordion player at the age of eight; winner of countless Fleadh Cheoil competitions at age ten; and seasoned veteran of countless Irish radio broadcasts and concerts in his early teens. By the the time Paul was sixteen he had crossed the Atlantic to make solo appearances on the Ed Sullivan and Perry Como television shows and major concert appearances at the legendary jazz venues the Roseland Ballroom, New York, with the Artie Shaw and Glenn Miller Orchestras and the Copacabana with Johnny Mathis. There are few other traditional players of any colour or creed that can boast of the same eventful, colourful musical life.

During his twenties and thirties, Paul's reputation as a top-rated accordion player was consolidated as a solo performer and with duet work with De Danann fiddler Frankie Gavin, with whom he produced one of the classic fiddle-accordion albums (*Omós do Joe Cooley—Tribute to Joe Cooley*) and regular session playing with most of Ireland's most celebrated traditional musicians. The last few years have seen this reputation gain even further with the release of a solo album *Mo Chairdín* (Gael-Linn) and the founding of The Moving Cloud Céilí Band, a band now in great demand among set-dancers who recognise superb players and a great céilí band when they hear one.

Paul Brock was born in the town of Athlone in 1944 and grew up in the pre-television era of battery radio, wind-up gramophone and 78 RPM records. It was through these that he absorbed his early love of music and in particular his early interest in traditional music. "Neither of my parents actually played traditional music," Paul remembers, "though my father had a keen interest in singing, especially the Irish tenors—John McCormack and all the big name singers of the era—and he sang around the house continuously. I suppose that was my first influence."

Though Paul did not know it at the time, there was around his home town a healthy Irish music fraternity to which he would soon be introduced. One of this number, Frank Dolphin, a regular visitor to the Brock household, was to play a vital role in Paul taking an interest in the music and later acquiring an instrument and developing his burgeoning, natural playing talent. His first instrument was the harmonica and he began to work out tunes he had heard over the radio. His introduction to the accordion came at the age of seven or eight, after a visit to his uncle's shop, where he was much taken with the instrument displayed in the shop window:

"I asked my uncle if I could look at it. He took it from the window and I took to it the instant I laid hands on it." Afterwards he knew he just had to have an accordion, and after much canvassing at home, Paul's father finally purchased one from a neighbour. "It was an ancient one-row Hohner melodeon and it came wrapped up in old newspapers. It cost my father a pound, but it got me started."

Frank Dolphin's timely appearance in Paul's life was crucial to his musical education and development. Paul is fulsome in his praise for Frank Dolphin's vital role in shaping his early musical education and his playing technique and imparting to Paul his general philosophy with regard to the playing of traditional music.

"Frank took me under his wing; he became my guru, I suppose. He played fiddle and accordion and I got my initial repertoire from him. The first tune I learned from Frank was a jig, *Saddle the Pony*, a great jig I still play." Frank imparted to Paul much more than a solid grounding in technique as well as the phrasing, expression of tunes. He was to instil in Paul a love and deep appreciation for the music made by the older players, such as the great Sligo fiddlers Michael Coleman, James Morrison and Paddy Killoran. In particular, Frank was to introduce him to the vast wealth of recorded material on 78s issued by the legendary accordion greats from the early part of the century, John Kimmel, Peter J Conlon and later, Joe Derrane. This love and deep appreciation of older musicians, their repertoires and above all, their stylistic approach to music, is at the heart of Paul's own personal musical philosophy. It also served to shape, in no small way, his own unique style of accordion playing.

Following Paul's rapid advances as a player under Frank Dolphin's watchful eye, he was soon to gain recognition, first locally and later around the country, as a young musician of exceptional talent. This was the era of the céilí band and Paul's exposure to some of the great bands of the day, the Aughrim Slopes, the Ballinakill, the Tulla and the Kilfenora, was maximum. At this stage his appetite for music was virtually insatiable; practically to the exclusion of all other youthful pastimes and pursuits. From the regular traditional music programmes on radio he soaked up the weekly diet of players, tunes and styles and then of course, there was the testing of ones musical metal at the Fleadh Cheoil competitions. In the Fifties, it was common for practically every traditional musician in the country to participate in Fleadh Cheoil local and national competitions. After walking away with every award at every competition, Paul Brock's reputation as an accordionist grew daily. A series of concert performances and radio broadcasts followed, which ultimately led to his being invited to play in America. There, at age sixteen, he played solo slots on several national television shows (as mentioned earlier), and even appearances with Artie Shaw and the Glenn Miller Band, two of the all-time great swing-jazz orchestras, at the Roseland Ballroom, surely the first time Irish traditional music resonated through the confines of that legendary and hallowed world-famous jazz venue. While proud of those concerts, Paul is modest, almost dismissive, about those achievements: "I enjoyed it, naturally, as I love jazz. I've had two musical lives. That was one of them. I don't really dwell on that period."

During these years—the early Sixties—his musical horizons had broadened; mainly due to his exposure to other virtuoso accordion players from Europe. One of these was the Norwegian genius of the accordion, Toralf Tolaffson. "I went to see Tolaffson perform live in Dublin in the Theatre Royal. He popularised the box in a way that few had before him. For me then, he was the maestro—a really big name. I met him later in London. He heard me play and encouraged me a lot and as a result, I went from a two-row to a three-row accordion." Other influences at this time were the French mussette players such as Medard Farrero and some Scottish players, such as the celebrated Will Starr, who played Athlone Town Hall in the Sixties.

Soon after his eighteenth birthday, he took the decision not to pursue the often insecure, often precarious career of life on the road as a professional musician.

Not that the playing stopped. His growing appetite for playing, particularly session playing, led Paul to sit in the company of the crême-de-la-crême of Irish traditional players at countless get-togethers the length and breadth of the country. He had at this stage moved to Clare to take up a job with Shannon Development Company, and immediately immersed himself in the rich musical culture of the county, playing with musicians such as fiddlers Dónal O'Connor from Kerry and Séamus Connolly from east Clare or the late Ciarán Collins, a gifted whistle player from Gort in south Galway. His tastes continued to broaden, extending to classical and American jazz. "I was hooked! Every penny I got went on travelling to London to see the visiting American jazzmen of the era. I saw some of the greats—Thelonious Monk, Miles Davis, Bill Evans— especially Bill Evans. If I saw Bill Evans was playing Ronnie Scott's Club in London, I just had to get to see him." When he wasn't chasing jazz concerts or studying classical guitar (yet another serious musical interest), he was to be found playing his accordion in all parts of Clare and south-east Galway.

It was at such a session in 1971 in Luke Kelly's pub in Gort that Paul Brock first met the teenaged fiddle virtuoso,

Frankie Gavin. He recalls, "I hadn't heard him play before, but right away I knew that here was a force to be reckoned with. He was something special." Paul had gone to see and hear the legendary Joe Cooley, who had recently returned from the United States, play one of his regular weekly gigs. Some time during the evening Paul and Frankie got an opportunity to play together and almost immediately, the musical chemistry between the two players fused, sparked and ignited. It was a spark that was to light their musical partnership for over fifteen years; right throughout the Seventies and Eighties. When Frankie Gavin wasn't touring or recording with the group De Danann, he more than likely could be found in Paul's company in some Clare or Galway music-pub, his fiddle matching Paul's accordion in a musical union that crackled with fire, passion and virtuosity. Their musical rapport was uncanny. Together, when they hit form, their instruments probed the depths and the heights of each tune. Each complex twist, each subtle turn, each delicate nuance was savoured and executed with both deadly speed and absolute accuracy as they teased, tested and shaped the possibilities of every tune to fit their inner vision of the music being played. The resulting music was breathtaking in its range of expression, exuberance, imaginative execution and sheer release of creative energy. The electricity of those Brock-Gavin performances are still remembered today. Joe Galligan, well-known organiser of one of the best-known folk and traditional clubs in Crusheen in Clare in the Seventies and Eighties, recalls the duo's regular visits to his club. "They were simply devastating. I've never heard fiddle and accordion played like that. I remember one night the music created such excitement, I though the audience would run wild. I'll never forget that night! Certainly their prowess as a fiddle-accordion duet has rarely been matched, before or since. I love the sound of fiddle and accordion. I think as instruments they fit well together."

The Brock-Gavin musical relationship is nowhere better captured than on their tribute album to Joe Cooley (a musical hero to both players), *Ómós do Joe Cooley* (Gael-Linn), released in 1986. Since then the album has entered the pantheon of traditional albums regarded as classics of the genre. Indeed, one critic voted it Traditional-Folk Album of the Decade. Certainly it stands as a milestone of fiddle-accordion recording that will stand the test of time. It remains an album Paul is justly proud of. He is proud too of his first solo album, *Mo Chairdín* (Gael-Linn), which was recorded and released in 1992, again to high critical acclaim. One of the high-points of that album is his evocative playing of the old piece, *The Blackbird*, on a 10-key Castagnari melodeon. The tune was recorded originally in 1910 by the great American accordion player and prolific recording artist John J Kimmel, a player whose work Paul has greatly admired and collected down the years.

These days, one of the most satisfying aspects, and chief interest, of Paul's musical life is his involvement with The Moving Cloud, a band he co-founded with fiddlers Maeve Donnelly and Manus McGuire, banjo player Christy Dunne and pianist Carl Hession. In early 1993, Christy Dunne was replaced in the band by Kevin Crawford, a gifted young musician whose reputation as a flute player of exceptional talent is already well established among his peers. The Moving Cloud's own reputation as a hot band—both with dancers and listeners alike—grows with the passing of each day.

Notes from the Heart

Throughout all his recorded and live work, Paul Brock's total love for, commitment to and mastery of, the music he plays with generosity of spirit, soulful subtlety, grace and depth of feeling is abundantly evident at all times. These are qualities which lie at the heart of traditional music at its very best. These are rare qualities, gifted to only a handful of musicians. Paul Brock is such a musician, as the listener can appreciate when witnessing his expressive, eloquent accordion in full flight, playing the music he was obviously born to play.

Discography:

Ómós do Joe Cooley/Paul Brock and Frankie Gavin (Gael-Linn CEF CD 115).
Mo Chairdín/Paul Brock (Gael-Linn CEF CD 155).
The Sound of Stone/Various Artists (BAGCD 001).